The South is Round

The South is Round

Contemplations of a
Twenty-first Century Redneck

David Magee

jefferson press

ISBN 978-0-977808-62-5
Library of Congress Catalog Card Number: 2006939886

Editing by Henry Oehmig
Cover Design by Jerry Dorris
Book Design by Fiona Raven

First Printing April 2007
Printed in Canada

Published by Jefferson Press

jefferson press

P.O. Box 115
Lookout Mountain, TN 37350

Some names, places and characteristics
have been changed, for obvious reasons.

*Being a newspaper columnist
is like being married to a nymphomaniac.
It is great for the first two weeks.*

—LEWIS GRIZZARD

*The North isn't a place.
It's just a direction out of the South.*

—ROY BLOUNT JR.

Contents

Introduction

I WILL AGREE WITH MOST aspects of the contemplative, articulate assumption made by Thomas Friedman in his bestselling book that the 21st century world is flat. Leveled in many parts by such forces as cheap, ever-present telecommunications that make talking to someone in rural China easy and the global outsourcing of manufacturing and services by domestic companies, the economic world according to Mr. Friedman is now navigable by anyone with a rugged entrepreneurial spirit and a good pair of walking shoes.

He argues in *The World is Flat: A Brief History of the Twenty-first Century* (Farrar, Straus and Giroux) that because of accessible and readily available technology and the shifting of jobs, people and intellectual property from one region to the other, the globe as we formerly knew it has been flattened to a figurative pancake's dimensions. Thus, cultural and geographic barriers are removed as hindrances to commerce and homogeneous growth.

Educated at Brandeis University and St. Anthony's College at the University of Oxford in England and serving as a columnist for The New York Times, Mr. Friedman is a renowned authority of world affairs who should know. If he says the world is flat, then I must agree—for the most part, at least. I don't question, for example, that the world lies at the hands of a creative, Chinese-speaking American, nor do I question that India's ability to provide cheap and on-the-spot technology and tech services which makes the country far more accessible to the rest of the world.

Anyone who knows or has lived for long in the South, however, understands that it is largely a world existing in itself—alienated from other regions and people by its own unique habits, traditions and imbedded cultures. To be sure, it's not the same backwards place that made negative national headlines in the 1960s, nor is it the unassuming, sleepy hollow it was in the 1970s and 1980s. Affluent minorities can now get a *reasonably* fair trial in most states, and school is no longer let out for half a day when a new McDonald's opens in town.

Areas of significant urban cultural flair can even be found these days from Memphis to Atlanta to Nashville to Charlotte, with smaller pockets sprinkled throughout from Little Rock, Arkansas to Tupelo, Mississippi to Montgomery, Alabama. In these places, it is not uncommon for fashionistas wearing Donald Pliner shoes to date boys who sip espresso while listening to Bela Fleck on their iPod, just as it is not uncommon for married couples to dress their toddler in tiny pairs of authentic Ugg boots in winter.

Just call them the Beverly (Georgia) Hip-billies.

Yes, the South has changed.

For example, many white people flaunted the derogatory word "nigger" in my youth, even if their intentions were well meaning. One might say, "Don't throw those clothes out—let's give them to the niggers." Or, another might say, "That nigger woman raised all those kids and not one of them has ever spent a day in prison." Today, however, almost no white person I know uses the word, but oddly, some black people do, particularly those of the younger generation.

I recall being at a high school track meet in middle Tennessee last year when several black teenagers seated in the bleachers next to me used the word with such frequency I was stunned. They were talking about and cheering on

. . . . . a black classmate who was running in a quarter-mile race
against a mostly-white field.

"That nigger sure can run," said one to the other.

"He damn sure can," said another, raising his voice. "Go
on, nigg-ah."

"Yeah, that nigger be too fast," chimed another, loudly.
"Damn."

The word sounded so powerful and romantic as it
repeatedly rolled from their tongues, through their lips
that I found myself fighting the urge to jump up and cheer
along with them at the top of my lungs.

"Run, nigger, run! Take out those honky boys!"

I thought better of screaming this, however. It would
insult all of the white people sitting nearby.

Yeah, the South has changed, but despite any examples
of contemporary metamorphoses—from increased harmony and tolerance to urban, Manhattan-style flair—it is
still is a land based on unrivaled idiosyncrasies. Where else
are there doctors named Bubba, girls doing chores on the
farm while wearing Seven jeans, and adults getting their
first taste of salmon (pronounced S-A-L-m-o-n) during
a wild and crazy whim at Outback Steakhouse? It is my
assumption, therefore, that this land mass that lies below
the Mason-Dixon Line is still as round today as the greater

world was when Christopher Columbus reported this finding to his king and queen in the late 1400s.

Educated at the other Oxford—the home of the
University of Mississippi—and as a columnist for the Chattanooga, Tennessee Times Free Press, I should not know.
In fact, just after Thomas Friedman finished mastering in-
depth thinking and global knowledge during his study in
England, I was struggling through a four-year education
at Ole Miss. Lack of high-brow knowledge aside, though,
I do have a bit of experience on my side, considering that I
was born in Louisiana, raised in Mississippi and currently
live in Tennessee. In reality, that probably only makes me
dumb, dumber and dumberer, not even taking into account
the fact that I also married a girl from Arkansas and once
owned a pair of camouflage boxer underwear.

One never knows when he might be caught half-naked
in the woods and needing to conceal his mid-torso.

Nonetheless, I am completely willing to share my insight
as a lifelong, redneck child of the South trying to make sense
of his place and space in the twenty-first century because it
is extremely important, following times of change, to give
pause, reflecting and analyzing where exactly it is we stand.
Without a doubt, that is what Mr. Friedman effectively did
with his book in reference to the world, helping to frame

the driving economics of the new century. It sold more than one million copies.

Good as his book may be, though, it ignores from my shameless point of view the fact that there are in reality multiple worlds in our global universe. Among the most distinctive is this land on which I was birthed and on which I have struggled to maintain footing on its sloping surface for more than 40 years since. Driven not by economics as the rest of the world, the South is shaped, molded and motivated instead by a host of social nuances including, to name a few, vanity, mild insanity, football scores, criss-crossed politics, birthright and a man's ability to cook a turkey on the grill.

And, while it is a land that changed substantially as it morphed with the rest of the world into the 21st century, few will question that it is still very much a place unique in its own right—to the point of complete and utter distinction. No, the new, new South is not flat; it is unquestionably, unfortunately, unequivocally, unapologetically and abso-lutely round. My intention, then, is to try and make sense of why this is so, just as Mr. Friedman did in context to the larger world.

Of course, I don't expect this book to sell one mil-lion copies. How many people really care, anyway, that the contemporary Southern girl no longer sits when she smokes or that most roadside produce stands these days are just fakes? Still, my contemplations, based on a mix of personal experiences and observations of others, are offered in hopes that each backwards step we Southerners have taken forward into this 21st century can be better misunderstood.

Chapter One

•
•
•
•
•

We're All Still Rednecks at Heart

WHEN I WAS A CHILD growing up in the South in the late 1960s and early 1970s, there was a certain understanding among most people living in the region that a dividing line existed between us and the somewhat-progressive rest of the world. It didn't matter that I lived in a small college town where half of the population possessed a college degree and perhaps one-third at least knew who Charles Bukowski was. We were no different in Oxford, Mississippi than residents of Itta Bena, Mississippi; Americus, Georgia or Bogalusa, Louisiana.

Most automobiles did not have air-conditioning, the nation's interstate system was still under development, and seat-belts were a nuisance that had to be removed by scissors. These, among other reasons, made travel and exploration difficult and kept our small, rural worlds generally closed off from the fad movements in taste and culture sweeping from California to New York. Ranch dressing, for example, was revered in the Golden State for 10 years or more after its creation in Hidden Valley before Southerners caught on, slathering the new, creamy ketchup over everything from salads to baked potatoes as well as each other.

Our clothes were mostly ordered from Sears or J.C. Penney catalogues—and I'd still wear those Toughskin jeans today, but give me one each in red, green and blue—because getting to a metropolitan mall was too much of a chore. Even if we did manage a trip, the choices were more along the lines of Fred Rogers' taste than Paul McCartney's, keeping a thin, denim line of distinction between backwoods dwellers and sophisticates of the South. As a result, about the only difference between Billy Bob and Bobby Sue Have and Bobby Bill and Sue Bobby Have Not, is that the Haves drove a big, new Buick and possessed a fondue pot and skewers. The Have Nots, on the other hand, drove an older model car and had little more to show for modern times than a shellacking kit and a needle and thread for macramé.

"That's a beautiful purse you've made, babe. How'd you get that hard, shiny finish?"

But along with the approach of the 21st century came the fluid movement of people. Due to better roads and transportation as well as the increase of wealth in the region, Southerners began to peek beyond their previously limited horizons just as Northern savants began to look for opportunities among our fertile grounds. The outcome was that by the time I was a 30-something, professional father of three at the turn of the century, I had joined hordes of others in believing we had left our rural and backwards beginnings behind.

There were rednecks, and then, there were the rest of us.

They continued to dine on potted meat, while our attention was focused on places like a favorite groovy, bamboo-fortified dive where patrons nibbled on salted edamame and chatted above loud, funky beats, while waiting on orders of fresh sashimi and designer rolls. Sure, we all shopped at the same Wal-Mart together, by necessity, but that's as far as interaction went. We, on the other hand, jetted to New York for long weekends of shopping. Yes, that woman strolling through the store while holding her Prada bag and wearing her Gucci sunglasses and Juicy Couture jeans is actually from Paducah, Kentucky.

"Ya'll can't touch this," she's thinking to herself.

Life has a way of bringing us back to reality, however, and it was during a particularly odd set of events in my life a few years ago that prompted me to theorize that, while it seemed everything about the South had changed; in reality, it was nothing more than a wrinkle in the Toughskin fabric of our region.

The first of these measures began on a gray January day in northern Mississippi, with air cold enough to make the tips of uncovered fingers hurt, but just warm enough so that light drops of falling moisture reached the ground as rain, not sleet. My friend, Bart, had been back at work for just long enough after New Year's Day that all of his guilt for pre-holiday blow off had evaporated, and the realization of the long and arduous tasks ahead had sunk in. It was after lunch on a Tuesday when the telephone rang.

"You want to go hunting?" Bart said.

"Today?"

"I'll pick you up in 30 minutes."

"I can't. I've got stuff to do."

"Like what?" he said. "Listen, you haven't killed a deer yet this season. I'm going to take you out and let you do all the shooting. I'll just watch 'cause I don't care anything about killing a deer today."

With three bucks already in the freezer and considering that he did not much like the taste of venison anyway, my friend said he was merely looking for something to occupy the time of his goof from work. Besides, he said, he would

be in his work clothes and car and didn't want to have anything to do with a deer himself. A territorial salesman, he
almost always dressed casual enough so that any canceled
appointment or sudden bout of boredom could be parlayed
into a round of golf or an armed jaunt through the woods
on a moment's notice.

"Fine," I said, relenting. "Pick me up."

From the front window of my house, I saw Bart's company, gray Ford Taurus pull up the driveway. I meandered
out the door—blaze orange hat on my head, a loaded .270
rifle in one hand, soft drink in the other. At the car, I placed
the rifle on the roof, cracking open the door.

"I forgot to tell you," I told him. "I've got a meeting
tonight and have to be back home by 5:00."

"Just throw your shit in the backseat and get in before
somebody sees us," Bart barked.

We drove fifteen minutes on a four-lane highway, head-
ing east from downtown Oxford. It was misting lightly
when we pulled off the road and arrived at the entrance to
the hunting spot. As we stepped out of the car, our feet sank
in the soft, old logging road, becoming caked with mud.
Realizing he would need to return home in the appearance of having had a day's work, Bart walked to the rear of
the Taurus, popped the trunk, and pulled the appropriate
boots from a pile of clutter that looked mostly like sales

brochures and order forms. He put on the boots, grabbed a rifle, loaded it, and closed the trunk.

"Let's go," he said.

Together, we began our march into the hunting grounds, which promised to take 20 minutes or more on foot. With my hat pulled down low to shield the cold spray that, more than rain, looked like remnants of an aerosol can being discharged from in the sky, I watched the ground as we proceeded...one step, two steps, three steps. However, before my foot hit the ground on the fourth, I was frozen by an ear-splitting shot.

BAM!!!!

Startled and momentarily disoriented, I raised my head to see my friend, standing not more than three feet away, still poised in the shooting position like a golfer staring down a well-struck seven iron. A glance toward his feet revealed the spent cartridge.

"What the hell was that?"

"That, my friend, was an eight-point buck hitting the ground."

"What?" I said, keeping my voice two octaves higher than normal. "You just killed a buck? I thought I was going to shoot the deer."

"You were," Bart said, "but I couldn't help it. I looked

over in that tall grass, and his horns were sticking up. It was just instinct, ya know?"

We walked over to the deer and stood over it a few minutes. My friend prodded it a few times with his gun barrel to make sure it was dead. Then he waited for a moment and nudged it again, amply satisfied that the buck had died completely and wasn't going to get away. The light mist turned to steady rain. We grabbed the buck by its horns, dragging it less than 60 yards to the car. There, my friend assessed his options.

"Hmmm."

Pulling keys from his pocket, he stroked the button which opens the trunk on the keyless pad.

Pop.

Bart walked over and looked inside the trunk, before shoving boxes of sales brochures and materials back and to the left.

"Guess it is going to have to go in here."

Without a blanket to cover the interior of the trunk, he grabbed some three-paneled sales brochures from one box and spread them out, hoping they would prevent the blood dripping from the deer's bulleted neck from staining the car. We grabbed the buck by its legs, hoisting it into the trunk. The hind quarter wouldn't fit, so my friend placed his back on it and shoved, grinding with power from his thighs, until the deer was encapsulated safely and presumably comfortable in the Taurus.

Slam.

After snickering all along the way back down the highway at the thought of having an eight-point buck in the trunk of the company car in the middle of a work day, we arrived at a small, somewhat-dilapidated trailer that had a sign out front fashioned from cut ply board and red spray paint, pronouncing, "WE CLEAN DEER." Standing in front of the trailer was a large man, obviously the proprietor. He had a scruffy beard and wore overalls covered with a red-stained white apron. He peered at the now-parked car.

"Roll down the window and tell the man we've got a deer over here," Bart said.

"Oh, I get it. You're embarrassed you've got a buck in the trunk, right?"

"Look at that big Man Mountain Link-looking motherfucker," Bart said, raising his voice. "I'm not telling that redneck to come to over to my Taurus to get a deer. What's he going to think?"

Exasperated and ready to get back home in plenty of time for my meeting, I opened the door and approached the man.

"Sir, we've got a deer that needs cleaning."

"Awwight. Where is it?" he asked.

I motioned to Bart to pop the trunk. He did, and I escorted Man Mountain Link over. He took a deep look into the back of the Taurus, scratching his head.

"I spec it'll be about $50 dollars to clean this buck and make your sausage, hamburger and steaks. I'll just pull the loin off straight. It'll be ready by next Wednesday to the noon hour. We take cash only."

"Okay," I told him.

Man Mountain Link grabbed the deer by its front legs and gave a mighty pull, easily removing it from the car, but spreading blood on the interior of the trunk as thickly as I imagined he buttered the inside of his biscuits. But the deer was out of our hands now and into his, so we headed on our way home.

"What did he say about that?" Bart inquired.

"Nothing," I said. "Absolutely nothing. And that's a problem."

"Why?"

"Because," I said, "that wasn't the first deer in the trunk of a company car that man has seen."

Before the events of this day, I had already begun to theorize on the notion that, no matter how much culture we Southerners believe we have acquired, we are all still rednecks at heart. It was a supposition along the lines of,

-
-
-
-
-

you can take the boy from among the rednecks, but you will never be able to take the redneck from the boys.

After being exposed by Man Mountain Link that we were more common than ingenious, I was moving ever-closer to the conclusion that we are all rednecks after all. Still, I was holding onto to the outside hope that some of us could escape the clutches of the white, roughneck heritage that clings through generations like eggs to an un-greased, black-iron skillet. However, one hot day on a golf course just south of Memphis, some six months after hav-ing helped place a deer in the trunk of a company-owned Taurus, my hypothesis that an innate redneckedness exists in all Southerners was put to a serious, discerning test.

The same friend who had called in January to take me hunting called again in July to see if I wanted to play golf in a two-man scramble tournament, to be held in Memphis the next day. Bart had signed up to play with someone else, but that person could no longer get off work and play. My handicap was double digits, but due to a lifestyle as a full-time writer, my work-day commitment calendar was clear, making me the ideal fill-in candidate.

"Great," he said, "I'll pick you up at 7:00 a.m."

An hour drive from Oxford and located on the east side of Memphis, the course we were to play was relatively new but had a layout that promised quality play. We arrived in time to warm up, hitting balls on the range among the more than 70 golfers participating. While attempting to properly strike two dozen or so balls, a sharply-dressed, middle-aged man, who professed to be a Tennessee lawyer by trade and a golfer by passion, warmed up on my left.

Wearing a white ball cap with a Titleist logo, a white, sleeveless sweater pulled over a silky blue shirt, soft, khaki slacks and a thick copper bracelet clasped tightly around his right wrist, he smoothly swatted one ball after another, oblivious to the heat which was already pushing toward the upper 90s.

"I love this game," he said. "It's the purest sport man ever invented."

To my right was a young man who appeared to be in his early 20s. Wearing wrap-around, designer sunglasses, an Auburn University cap, a collar-less golf shirt and baggy shorts, he ripped one 300-yard drive after another, leaving every club but his driver untouched during practice. Upon noticing that I was more concerned watching him from the corner of my eye than I was with my own shots, the young man reached out to me in words.

"You the Magee team?" he inquired.

"Yep. That's me."

"Cool," he said. "They told me that we were paired with you. That's my dad, there, right beside you.

"What's your handicap?" he asked.

I didn't have the heart to tell him the truth—that I had no idea, and that an educated guess would place it at 20 or more.

"Fourteen."

"Cool," he said. "I'm a six. Dad's a four. He gets to play more than I do."

Great. Bart was a scratch, but golf is pretty much a stand alone game, even in a team format. A pairing with Slick and Super-Slick spelled misery for me all day long. But, I was in Memphis, on the course and fully warmed up. Unable to turn back, I shuffled into the cart just before 9:30 a.m. and rode to the second hole, our starting point for the shotgun format. Waiting at the tee upon our arrival was the father and son, our playing partners.

"You boys like to have fun?" the man inquired. "I hope so, 'cause I plan on having some fun today. I'm out of the office and my motto is, 'screw everything else.' You know what I mean?

"Today, it's all about birdies 'n beer. You know what I'm saying?"

He reached into his cart and removed a can, pulling the tab.

Pssshhht.

Gulp, gulp, gulp.

"Ahhhhh.

"Let's play some golf, boys."

The man was not that much older than my friend and I, really. At the most, he had 12 years on us, and many of my friends were his age or older, but I yielded in the beginning to his take-charge, parental style because it seemed he liked it best that way. The longer we played, however, the more difficult this became.

Before finishing our seventh hole of play we had been approached a couple of times already by two blonde, 20-something flirtatious girls driving the beer cart. Each time they stopped, the man and his son grabbed an armload of beers. By the completion of our ninth hole and still before noon central daylight time, the man had consumed nine beers by my count; same for the son. But it was Daddy doing all the talking.

To the beer girls, he made suggestive small talk each time they visited, uttering such phrases as, "ya'll sure are cute" and, "sure, you can help me, any time you want." To my friend and me, he unleashed from tee box to fairway to green an increasingly steady stream of male-centric questions.

"You boys like (vagina), don't ya?" he asked.

"Uh, yes sir," I said feebly, nodding toward Bart. "We like (vagina). Sure do."

Of course, the more beer the man and the boy drank, the worse their golf became. Our team was four shots under par after the first nine holes, while they were just one under, despite having started with three birdies in the first three holes. In the sweltering summer heat, hovering in the high 90s, and halfway through the round of golf, all the beer the father and son had consumed started talking loud and clear in regards to their game.

Thump.

The man chunked into the ground a six-iron, one of the clubs that he had struck so effortlessly on the practice range. Instead of lifting off, the ball only hopped and skidded along, but kept rolling nonetheless, finding its way, somehow, to the edge of the green.

"I call that a vagina shot," the man slurred. "You know, it looks awful, but leaves you feeling pretty damn good."

At the 12th hole, the beer cart girls met up with our foursome once again, waiting for us all to hit tee shots before initiating discussion.

"Can we get you anything?" the girl driving asked.

"Yeah, baby," the man responded, while looking at us and capping it with a slight wink. "You can get me something. How about a peek at those breasts of yours?"

Giggle.

Something had come over the girls, I could immediately

tell. Dressed identically in tight blue jean cutoffs and white
tank tops with thin bra straps showing, they had crossed
over from the playful enticement that comes naturally in
service work, into a sort of sloppy sprawl of lechery. They
were the Drs. Jekyll and Misses Hyde of beer cart babes,
and the transformation was underway.

"Have you girls been hitting the beer?" I said.

Giggle, giggle.

"Naaawwww," one finally replied, somewhat gruffly.
"The *beer* has been hitting *us*."

The man could not resist the opening.

"We'd like to hit on you, too."

Our foursome continued playing, despite the rapid
deterioration of the father and son, who were now making
a day out of bogies and beer, and the girls followed us for
another two holes, popping tops all along the green-grass
way. Then, one's cell phone rang. It turned out that a golfer
on another hole was summoning the girls for beer delivery.
They left us, pledging in a slur to soon return.

Although my friend and I had not consumed even a
sip of beer, we didn't think it odd that one of the girls
had given out her cell phone number to a tournament
golfer. We did, however, find that our play had flattened
out to mediocrity due to the distractions. The summer
sun was bearing down painfully as the clock reached mid-

•
•
•
•
•
•

afternoon. Sweat dripped from every conceivable part of our bodies.

"I wish this would hurry up and end," Bart barked.

As we reached our 16th hole of play, the actual 17th hole on the course, the already-odd day took an unusual, if not memorable, swerve. Running 380 yards and parallel to a busy, two-lane state highway, number 17 was a straight shot layout in view of all driving to the golf club, or anyone traveling to destinations east or west. From the tee box, my friend ripped a drive 290 yards down the left, leaving his ball just next to the cart path and within 30 yards of the adjacent highway.

Standing over his ball and marveling at the shot, we talked as best as we could with the inebriated father and son, waiting for the group ahead to leave the green so we could approach. Drs. Jekyll could be heard approaching from the rear, singing songs playing on a newly-found radio.

"*Celebrate good times, come on!*," they sang, bump, bump, bumping along every pothole and course indention on the way.

"Heeeeyyyyyy," the passenger of the beer cart managed to say upon arrival. "What do ya'll want?"

Recognizing, perhaps, that the golf tournament was quickly coming to an end, the man hopped from his cart, not wasting a moment to respond.

"What do we want?" he said. "What do we *want*?

"I'll tell you what we want. We want to see you eat her (vagina). You hear what I'm saying? We want to see you eat her (vagina), right here and right now. That's what we want."

Silence.

I grimaced in the direction of Bart, my neck turning red in splotches with embarrassment.

"Don't mind him," I said to the girls, "he's just a drunk lawyer from Tennessee."

The beer cart girls were paying full attention, however.

"How much will you pay us?" the beer cart driver wanted to know.

"Twenty bucks," the man said.

"Forty."

"Deal."

Before I could process what was in the midst of transpiring, the girls bumbled out of the beer cart. They were standing and facing each other on the fringe of the 17th fairway, one car zipping closely by after another. Standing less than 10 feet away from the girls, neither my friend nor I uttered a word, figuring, I guess, that they would call bluff any moment.

Regretfully, they did not.

The passenger girl unbuttoned her blue jean shorts,

eased down the zipper to about halfway and hooked her thumbs within the left and right straps of a thin, white thong. She slid both down to her knees and squatted on the ground, smiling all the while. She then rolled onto her back, grabbing her legs behind the knees and pulled them toward her head. Absent of pubic hair and shyness, there were no obstructions of play—just a clear shot to the hole. The driver of the cart knelt to her knees, leaned in by bracing her arms against the passenger's legs, lowered her head, and proceeded to swish and swirl her tongue for what seemed like an hour, but must have lasted 90 seconds.

Nobody spoke a word.

After a few moments—however long they were—the driver girl stopped and stood, and the passenger girl quickly jumped up, pulling her shorts and undergarment snugly back into place. The girls turned in unison to the man and each held their hands out for a twenty dollar bill. He quietly deposited them along with a kind of high-five slap into their palms. Money in hand, the girls got back into the beer cart and fled, not leaving so much as a Michelob Ultra for the father and son.

The shots hit by our foursome on the ensuing two and a half holes were among the worst I've ever seen to this day. Bart and I said nothing of what we had witnessed; only occasionally shaking our heads in the direction of each other with half-smile smirks. On the hour's drive back home, my friend finally asked the question I knew we both were thinking.

"What in the world are we going to tell our wives?"

"Well," I said, after thinking for a moment. "We had nothing to do with that—at all. And, I don't think by any stretch of the imagination I can walk through the door, and, when my wife asks about the tournament, tell her that we had 13 pars, five birdies, a few laughs, and watched a girl with a shaved box get her (vagina) eaten on number 17."

"Let's just say we had fun," Bart said, "and never say another word about it."

"Agreed."

Bart dropped me off. Of course, my wife immediately asked about the day.

"It was okay," I said. "You know...just another scramble."

It was not until later, in a time of solitude that evening, when reflection on the day's the strange occurrence allowed me to properly piece it together with the deer in the trunk episode. I realized then that there are moments when we are so full of our contemporary, Southern selves that we may think that the redneck from which we were bred has been left far behind. The reality, though, is that only a redneck would in the same year, stuff a deer into the trunk of a company sedan and watch one girl lick another's vagina on the golf course. And, if this quality of redneckedness remained innately in me, as well as my friend, then, with little question, it still lies within every man and woman birthed and reared in Dixie, shopping trips to New York or a love of hip sushi restaurants be darned.

Chapter Two

She's So Fat, She's Gonna Blow

THE OLDER I GET, THE more dismayed I become with politicians on both sides of the right and left equation. With each passing year, it seems our country's elected officials become less creative and more legislatively boxed into the same few issues. No longer governed by Demublicans and Republicrats, we are now caught in the midst of a territorial battle between assholes and bigger assholes. On Election Day, this means we are often forced to cast a rather innocuous vote, choosing which person, and party, we would prefer to douse us with excrement.

> *Eenie, meenie, minie, moe,*
> *Catch a liar by the toe,*

.
.
.
.
.
.

If he hollers, let him go,
My mamma told me,
I would rather be,
Dumped on by…you!

(blacken in appropriate circle; or, in the case of Florida, weakly punch a chad.)

Then along came former Arkansas Governor Mike Huckabee, who reminded me a couple of years ago that our world is still okay because some elected officials actually do hold within their grasp the potential for unveiling original and non-political ideas and actually helping in a time of crisis. Recognizing that the South has been lured into a type of cold war by its northerly neighbors, who quietly try to ensure our 21st century demise by enticing us to gorge ourselves to death on junk food, including doughnuts and Doritos, Huckabee decided to counterattack. Call it the Battle of Magazine Mountain, his vision and courage to attack through both legislation and public relations one of the most pressing issues today facing the South and there-fore, his decidedly Southern constituency: our obese.

Once a portly 280-pounder, the two-and-a-half-term for-mer governor of the pork belly state slimmed to 177 pounds by losing weight the old fashioned way—eating less and exercising more. He told anyone who would listen how he had done it and urged them to do the same. More importantly, however, is the fact that he led his state to adopt in 2004 a Healthy Arkansas initiative, aimed at showing others the benefits of a healthy lifestyle which adds a low-fat, nutritious diet to exercise. So compelling was Huckabee's argument, that he actually got enough votes in the general assembly to pass Act 1220, legislation which directly tackles childhood obesity through public schools.

It was one thing, he must have figured, when one-third of the students in Arkansas public schools could not adequately read and write, but when third grader rear ends reached the size of watermelons grown around Monticello, well, something had to be done. As a result of Arkansas' schools obesity program, the Body Mass Index (BMI) of every student in the state's public system is now measured, and the results are sent home to parents as a type of report card. It is a plausible move, certainly, but one can only imagine the implications.

"Dear Mrs. Smith," the teacher writes, "I would like to inform you that for the semester, your daughter has two A's, two B's and one extremely super-sized derriere. Much improvement is needed in the latter area."

The day has come where obesity in the South is no laughing matter. From Mountain Home (Arkansas) to Mountain Brook (Alabama), people are getting larger, and larger and larger, falling prey to the quiet but destructive conflict that I suspect the North launched sometime before the news was revealed that Arkansas' own Bill Clinton fondled Monica Lewinsky's love organ with a cigar before spewing semen on her dress. And prior to the infamous banquet in which Mississippi's Trent Lott uttered a racially offensive remark when attempting to roast Strom Thurmond. With pre-scandal, all-powerful President Clinton leading the nation, and pre-slur, all-powerful Sen. Lott in control of the senate as majority whip, the Yankees undoubtedly feared the South was en route to taking over America, thereby creating a redneck nation. An offensive was undoubtedly launched, hurling sparkling new outlets of Krispy Kreme, outfitted with convenient, open-late drive through windows, and easy-to-use Wal-Mart Supercenters, also outfitted with operational bakeries positioned strategically near the front door, throughout the south by the dozens.

"I don't understand why I'm gaining all this weight, baby," one woman complains. "There must be something wrong with my thyroid, baby. I mean, all I ate today, baby, was two eggs and bacon, a Lean Cuisine, and some meatloaf and carrots off Cody's plate."

"Huh? What's that, baby? Well, no, I didn't count those 26 donut holes—they only took me six bites, baby. Yeah, that was a whole loaf of cinnamon bread I ate in the parking lot. But, I did not know you was looking."

It is not just Southern belles packing on the pounds, either. As farm and general labor jobs have evaporated and as more junk food, including 33 percent larger beef sticks and chicken-on-a-stick, is covertly pipelined into the region, our more sedentary males have packed on the LBs at the astonishing rate of grizzlies approaching hibernation. This is not to suggest that the group, as a whole, ever took great care. Fried foods have long been a passion and hobby of the Southerner, and even in these contemporary times, a girl getting married in Gwinnett County, Georgia, is still expected to choose a Fry Daddy to appear as a gift option on the wedding registry at Target.

Belles that try and buck the trend, in hopes of keeping their man in a 34-waist pair of pants, are often rebuked by well-intentioned friends, who presumably don't want to be in tow of the only bucket of lard at the next meeting of the young couples' dinner club six months down the road. One 20-something girl I know from Kentucky, who grew up on a farm but managed to avoid fried foods, said the peer pressure to give in at marriage was simply more than she could take.

"Girl, how can I get you a Fry Daddy when you haven't signed up for one?" her friend inquired.

"I can't sign up for a Fry Daddy when I don't even know what one is," she said.

"Well," the friend responded, "A Fry Daddy is how you keep your husband happy, girl. When he catches fish, they go in the Fry Daddy. When he kills some squirrels, roll 'em in batter and throw 'em in the Fry Daddy. When he wants some biscuits, get your Fry Daddy hot and just throw that dough in...you'll see what I mean, girl."

Yielding to the wisdom of her friend, who had been successfully married for five years, albeit to a man ever-increasing in girth, my friend signed up for a Fry Daddy. However, some nine months after marriage, my friend's husband was reportedly following the same path as her friend's husband. Still handsome in his 5-foot-8 frame, he was said to no longer be a lean, mean country boy machine that could boot-scoot and boogie. It was more slide by, slippety slide, I know I've gained 28 pounds, but can you throw some more of those chicken tenders in the Fry Daddy, please?

Even today's health-conscious Southern male can't stray too far from his roots and innate, preferred tastes. Sitting in a restaurant like, say, Bud and Alley's at Seaside, Florida, noted for its urban blend of flavors from coastal Mediterranean and the lowlands of Florida, I listen intently as men, who previously in the day jogged three miles, had a cup of espresso and read *The New York Times*, order sautéed fish. They seem to feel good about themselves, sipping on a glistening glass of pinot noir while asking for a white, flaky meal, but it is all I can do not to lean over and holler some eye-opening words, suggesting he might be just as happy sipping a fully-loaded Coke and hunkering down over a plate of fried marine life at Uncle Bud's in Selmer, not Bud and Alley's in Seaside.

"That's a fried fish, you fool. Why don't you just ask them to bring on out a basket of hushpuppies, some country-style potatoes, and a heapin' helpin' o' slaw along with it? You know you want it."

Most do want it, too, along with the doughnuts and Doritos, and it's taking a toll, collectively blowing up our region one rack of ribs at a time. That's why the political endeavor by former Gov. Huckabee makes so much sense. Never an advocate for government intervention in our lives—I don't think, for instance, that Twinkies or Oreos should be outlawed, or even taxed, like cigarettes. But some expansion of this educational effort, which began in Arkansas, might serve as an effective counter attack on this Cold War. A starting point might be to take the amount of dollars and approach used in the federal government's reportedly-successful anti-drug campaign, in which Uncle Sam urges teenagers to "Just Say No." Drugs are certainly a major problem, and more needs to be done, but obesity impacts far more people and probably costs us more in health care.

In Tennessee, as one example, a United Health Foundation report showed that in 2003, 60 percent of the state's residents were either overweight or obese. The report noted that, since 1990, the number of obese people living in Tennessee has doubled. This leads me to believe it is time for a new promotional campaign, so that Rocky Top and Neyland Stadium don't crumble under the burgeoning weight of the people.

This is your fat ass and redneck beer gut. This is your fatter ass and redneck beer gut on pork rinds.

There was hope, for a spell, when the low-carbohydrate craze swept the landscape that people would thin down for once and for all. Everybody, it seemed, was dropping carbohydrates from their diet and inches from their waistline. From Wilmington, North Carolina to Amarillo, Texas, pork rind sales soared, boiled peanuts came back en vogue, and steak consumption went from exceptionally high to outrageously high. So amazed was I at the reported results, that I tried a low-carbohydrate diet myself for eight months. Without a doubt, my BMI during the diet dropped to a more respectable level, minus a second chin, male breasts and a bulging stomach, which had been growing since the first day I enrolled at Ole Miss without a BMW. Make no mistake: If carbohydrates are not consumed in high quantities, you will definitely lose weight. But there are other hazards associated with the carbohydrate-less diet, like no lemon icebox pie and less-than-pleasant breath resulting from the burn-off of previously-stored fat.

"What did you have for lunch," my wife once inquired, "rotten goat?"

In response, I proceeded to eat a sandwich enveloped in plain white bread, chasing it with carbohydrate-loaded chips, followed by cookies. Sunbeam, Golden Flake and Mrs. Fields never tasted so good. And, except for minimal flirtations with the low-carbohydrate concept, I have never been back. Others apparently have followed suit, and it doesn't take reading the story about how Atkins Nutritionals, Inc., the company that soared during the low-carbohydrate craze, went bankrupt to know. Just go to the nearest indoor mall on a Saturday—any Saturday. It doesn't matter if you are in Hot Springs, Arkansas or Orlando, Florida.

Take your stance somewhere in the middle of the building, making sure your view isn't obstructed by one of those merry-go-rounds or Dippin' Dots stands. Look left, then right. Realizing that you can't see the Bath and Body Works for the traffic of big butts, you, too, will see that the low-carbohydrate phase is clearly over and that the majority

-
-
-
-
-
-

of people living in today's South are growing more robust than condo prices in Myrtle Beach.

Without a doubt, more needs to be done, before Dixie implodes altogether. But the removal of even one Fry Daddy from an addicted household is not easy, regardless of the location. Whether the obese live in hot, sticky Montgomery (Alabama), or cool-breeze Asheville (North Carolina), the job requires a highly-skilled professional, someone who can remain calm at all times, can be trusted in the tensest of situations, and will be true to the citizens, as well as to themselves.

Sounds to me like a job for a governor; or, an explosives expert.

Chapter Three

•
•
•
•
•

Meat Smoking Son of a Gun

I CALL THEM redneckosexuals, the small percentage of today's young, Southern males who feel that—by virtue of significant, six-figure earnings and a sort of uber-hipness learned from metropolitan travel and hyper-shopping and fashion conscious wives—they have the world by the tail, moving it and grooving it however and whenever. It's a blend of rural, generational toughness and soft, cosmopolitan self-enlightenment, dwelling in cities like Atlanta, Jacksonville, Memphis, Mobile, Nashville, Birmingham and the like.

The opposite of Manhattan's metrosexual male, who can rarely be identified by testosterone traits, the South's contemporary hip-billy is part Jethro and John Wayne mixed with an equal portion of Paris Hilton and Madonna. These

·
·
·
·
·

men are just as liable to sneak off from work early on a Friday to hunt ducks as they are to get a slight permanent and dye job for wilting, withering hair.

This young, savvy Southern male likely works as either a litigant lawyer, a specialist doctor, commodities broker, real estate developer or as a chairman's son inheritor, working out at the gym on his muscle tone during the lunch hour, sucking down three beers with the boys at the neighborhood bar during happy hour, driving either a fast-foreign car or a big America truck on the commute to work, and counting his accruing money at all hours.

He's always dressed in perfect coordination, whether its a Ralph Lauren suit complimented with a purple tie, or sporting Gucci loafers with a t-shirt and jeans, and, with the exception of the office, where the pressure to earn more, more, more never ends, or when his latest, greatest cell phone slash emailer slash music device slash address book slash microwave oven quits working, he is generally a nice guy, if for no other reason, he was taught by his congenial, homespun parents to be that way. And, he's got hobbies, too. Man, does he ever have hobbies. There are golf bags filled with the biggest of the big, bad drivers and the hottest new irons and a putter designed by former NASA engineers. There are shotguns and rifles, decks of cards, boats, skis—for water and snow—bows and arrows, yesterday's sports pages, tomorrow's sports pages, televisions everywhere, and more golf clubs than will fit into four bags. And topping it all off is his signature possession: that metal contraption that truly stokes the wood chips of his heart, relaxing him with its zesty mesquite incense—yes, I'm talking about that instrument of redneckosexual nirvana—the meat smoker slash barbecue grill.

Any upwardly mobile, married, 20-something Southern male, knowing the difference between Men's Journal and Sports Illustrated and worth his salt, owns at least one, and it's likely a favorite source of both pride and those rare-but-precious idle moments. A kind of, kiss-my-butt-honey-I-can't-do-chores-around-the-house-for-once-today-because-as-you-see-I'm-cooking-somethin'-on-the-grill-for-the-entire-mother-fucking-family type of hobby with strong psychological roots reaching back to the days when man hunted, literally, for all bestial foods that the family would then barbeque over their campfire slash smoker.

In other words, it serves as an excuse to relieve men of the seemingly more feminine chores of life, like changing sheets or picking up toys around the house on a Saturday morning. But it also serves as a type of exoneration from some of the questionably feminine preferences of lifestyle these same men enjoy, like hair permanents, spa days and manicures. The metrosexual has a non-gendered purse; the redneckosexual has his heavily-gendered smoker slash grill, and he's not afraid to use it.

The appliance of choice for the fortunate and the more informed is the big, oblong-shaped ceramic shell known as "A Big Green Egg." This smoker slash grill is revered by men-who-know throughout South. They trade secrets of recipes and their expert understanding of the apparatus from office to office, from corporation to corporation, and from supper club to supper club. When secretaries, or wives, see them cloistered in the corner, strutting in front of one another in that swagger of haberdashery, talking from the sides of their mouths and laughing while F-bombs drop like it's Pearl Harbor all over again, they might suspect the men are whispering tales of escapades with wild women, but in all likelihood, the boys are talking about how long they smoked their hens on Saturday.

"Man," says one of guys-who-know, "I got that bitch too hot. She was tipping off at seven hundred degrees, so, you know, I had to bring her on down, man. I eased that bitch on back to about 300, then, you know, I slid my chicken on in. In about four hours, my fucking bird was right, man. I mean right."

In my larger-than-life family, we are fortunate to have two reckneckosexuals by virtue of marriage—JT and

Frank, two of Atlanta's finest financial product brokers. Without question, the boys, as I call them, are the life of the group at gatherings and a source of my ever-amusement. And without question, what they talk about more than anything else is their beloved smoker slash grills and what they've barbequed most recently and what gadgets they've acquired to make their grueling job easier.

For example, I recall one recent Thanksgiving getting accidentally cornered by the boys when they were well past a few beers and a couple glasses of wine each. We were at JT's swanky lake house somewhere in Georgia. He was pointing to the water, explaining how with his new thermometer, he could actually get updated readings from his smoker slash grill while riding in his boat and pulling his precious little children on skis.

"That's some shit right there, isn't it?"

And, it was.

Because the boys are so adored by the family and because their passions impel them to take such action into their own hands, we began a few years ago to allow them to take over the big job of preparing the turkeys for family holiday gatherings. This is no small job, considering that often 35 or more relatives show up, expecting to be well fed. It is one thing to be responsible for bringing, say, wine. Just grab a handful of moderate priced bottles of anything red and rest assured that by mid-afternoon, it'll all be gone. The same can be said for mashed potatoes, broccoli casserole and the gravy; I've yet to see any go to waste. But turkeys are a different deal, because, for many years, we had an excellent cook, who reliably kept the family well fed before passing on and leaving us in need. The boys volunteered, and what were we to say?

The first year they were in charge, the turkeys came out okay, but the same couldn't be said for JT's car. With a big, new SUV in the driveway—back in the day when having a big, new SUV in the driveway was cool—JT was looking for a place to store his freshly-cooked turkeys for the night. He only had two breasts because it was to be a smaller-than-average gathering, but they were cooked the night before in hope of avoiding any first-time mistakes. With the breasts completely done by 11 p.m. and lunch some 13 hours away, he was off to a good start. But, since the birds were too large to fit into the refrigerator, he needed a place to keep them.

Considering that the forecast called for the temperature to be down in the forties overnight, the rooftop of the SUV seemed like a logical place. Of course, this was the logical answer. The turkeys would be refrigerated by nature and kept out of reach of his two, gifted Labrador retrievers. He had guessed right that the dogs couldn't reach the top of the car, but Mr. Redneckosexual failed to consider that the dogs might still want to at least try to get the bird breasts. Arriving the next morning, I couldn't help but notice that nearly all the paint had been scratched from the doors of the driver and passenger side of the cool, new SUV. In trying to reach the breasts, the dogs must have leapt one hundred times each toward the top, raking their claws back down the car every time.

"Guess I had better wait till morning to cook them next time," JT said.

Because the crowd anticipated for the family gathering the next year was three times as large and because JT didn't want to disappoint, he enlisted the help of Frank, his brother-in-law, who lived around the corner and who also had a smoker slash grill. The plan was that, in order to have enough bird for almost 40 guests, one person would cook two breasts, while the other would cook one extremely large whole bird. With experience in hand, JT took responsibilities for the breasts, advising Frank that he needn't start his big turkey until early in the morning the day of the event.

Shortly after lunch, JT arrived with his breasts—enough to feed one-third of the crowd gathered. One hour later, Frank arrived, urging the hostess to crank up her oven. Before it was even preheated, he plunged the bird in, wiping November sweat from his brow after the door closed.

"Give it an hour," he said.

"An hour!" I wanted to scream, "Have you any idea how hungry these people are?"

An hour and a half later, we had to carve the bird or starve the guests. For more than 20 minutes, Frank poked and prodded, searching for useable meat. The result was several large piles of finely chopped bird, akin to chopped pork at your favorite barbecue dive. The crowd ate, appreciative of the effort, and it was not until later in the day, when a first-time guest inquired if we "always chopped our turkey that way" that we realized how botched the bird had been.

Hoping that experience would prevail and not wanting to trample the boys' hearts by insulting their pride and joy, we let them attempt the birds yet another time. With the gathering slated for his house, JT, with the able assistance of Frank, was back on the job. Arriving early in the morning, I watched them work together, injecting some sort of flavored goop into the big turkey with the precision of an able-handed surgeon. Then, I watched them tend to the coveted smoker slash grill. Clad both in Gucci loafers and designer jeans, they poked and prodded the fire to perfection. Then turkey was placed inside and the valves closed down in the effort to get the temperature just right. The lid was never opened, but, throughout the day, the grill was

watched. I tried talking during this ritual, but found the
boys only half-listening, if at all.

"How's your baby girl?"

"What's that?" Frank responded. "Oh, great, great
man…look, she's just smoking along. That temperature is
holding tight."

"How's work?"

"It seems to be working okay," JT said, "but we might
need to add some wood chips."

But lo and behold, at 4:30 in the afternoon one turkey,
bronzed to perfection in the smoker slash grill, was brought
inside the house. Thirty minutes later it was carved and
served and to a person, it was loved. No comments about
chopped bird, no sweat dripping from the brow, just the
taste of succulent turkey.

This is not to suggest that these meat-smoking-son's-of-
guns mastered their greatest challenge, holiday meat, but
it is simply giving credit where credit is due. It will admit,
though, that the glory was short lived, considering that very
next year, JT overslept due to a bout with the cocktail flu
and did not get the turkey onto the smoker slash grill until
almost nine in the morning, making it a full three hours
late for the Thanksgiving party. And, it is true that, in an
effort to get the bird done faster, he ignored rule number
one, passed along from one redneckosexual to another in

a sing-song manner belted out to the tune of a popular Foghat rock song: *cook all meat slow and easy...*

The bird was so charred when JT brought it in to an empty table that, it appeared more like a relic abandoned in a house fire than something suitable for dinner. Standing nearby, Frank was so flustered that he was at a rare loss for words, unable, even, to utter a smart-ass remark. I could have sworn, in fact, that I saw what might have been a tear dribbling down his too-thin cheek. Turning away, I looked squarely at JT, who was struggling to hold the super-large, belatedly-done turkey on a platter. I could see the pain on his well-moisturized face, the furrowing of his neatly-plucked brows.

"Relax," I told him. "Christmas is just around the corner. Just refrigerate that thing on top of your car until then, and, for a change, you'll be a step ahead for the next gathering."

Chapter Four

•
•
•
•
•

What Was Wrong with Miller Beer?

IT WAS AN EARLY FALL day in 1980 that was, as I recall, hot enough to fry an egg on the parking lot asphalt. I was out of class at my junior high school an hour early, excused from the last period typically reserved for football practice because my team had a game later in the evening.

"Back here by 4:30," said the coach, in his final instructions, "ready to play."

The clock must have registered somewhere in the vicinity of 2:30 on the Thursday in memory. Two hours with nothing to do, except maybe wander to a nearby convenience store, choke down a soft drink, a few chicken legs and perhaps a pack of M & M's Peanut Chocolate Candies, before wandering back early and waiting for the rest of the team to gather in anticipation of the game. In no hurry, with nothing but time on my hands, I plodded on my own up the sidewalk which led from the school to the store, figuring that I would eventually reach my destination and ingest.

Not more than 200 yards away from my starting point, my walk was interrupted by three puny, little beeps of a car horn. I stopped and turned, seeing a small, purplish vehicle that looked more like something that should be stepped on than a car. Inside, I could faintly make out a driver through a window glaring under the searing sun. The driver was pumping one arm furiously from top to bottom, the result of which seemed to be lowering the window. I first saw short hair, then a kind-of-long nose, which pointed the way to a full-friendly smile.

"Hey, good lookin'," said the driver. "Whatcha got cookin'?"

Dana was the older sister of a female friend, who was one grade ahead of me and who attended another school. Before my friend could drive, Dana had given us rides to places like the movie, the skating rink and the ice cream shop. In reality, I wasn't especially close to the friend; she was more of a friend of a friend, but, she was nice. Not too cute and a little bit country, but nice. Her older sister, Dana, I knew barely at all, except for the loud talking she had done from the driver's seat a couple of times, and, the closeness with which she moved into my facial space as I squirmed in the passenger seat, trying to listen.

It was rumored that Dana was a third-year sophomore at an area junior college, who lived in a trailer trash home, commuting to classes some 40 miles away in her purple car. None of this mattered to me as she pledged while I stood on the sidewalk and her car idled in the street that she and a friend were driving around, looking for something interesting to do for the rest of the day. When I told her that I was walking to the store, killing time between then and 4:30, she summoned me to the car.

"Get in," she said. "We'll have you back in time."

Unsure if getting into the car alone with relatively strange college girls on a Thursday afternoon was a good idea, I hesitated.

'C'mon," she said. "Get in."

It did not matter that when I had seen her a few times before, one of her eyes was quite lazy, frequently crossing to face its rigid counterpart, or that she had smelled like cheap cigarette smoke and flashed teeth stained a light tinge of brown, or that her hips were slightly wide, or that she dressed from clothes that appeared to be purchased from a rack at the dollar store. She summoned, and I responded, walking toward the car and folding myself into something

•
•
•
•
•

akin to a pretzel, so I could squeeze into the back seat. In the car, I focused on Dana's more petite, less offensive friend positioned in the front, passenger seat.

"Hey," she said, "I'm Beth. So, you are going to Ben and Todd's with us?"

Even though I was still a junior high student, having imbibed nothing more potent than Milk of Magnesia, I knew that Ben and Todd's was an open-at-all-hours, sell-to-all-ages beer store run by a man named Ben and a man named Todd that was located just across the county line, almost 20 miles from our locale.

"Ben and Todd's, huh?"

"Yeah," Beth said. "We go there every day, you know... just to chill out and forget about everything we're supposed to be doing."

"Well, then. Ben and Todd's it is."

"We'll have you back in time," Dana said, stomping her large, right foot onto the car's gas pedal with such force that the engine's four-cylinders gave a short cough and choke, before kicking in enough horsepower to send us somewhat zooming away in a purple haze.

Threatened by 30 seconds of silence once the car's noise tapered off around 40 miles per hour, Dana grabbed an eight-track tape that she swore was bitchin'. With a little shove until it clicked into place in the player mounted into the dash, the tape started to play. She clasped the volume knob between her index finger and thumb and, giving it a twirl, exposed us to AC-DC's newly-released tracks. Onward we went toward Ben and Todd's, mesmerized by the first track's catchy lyrics that thumped from tiny, twin speakers. A high-pitched, screaming voice followed the loud, ominous sound of clanging bells, all accompanied by ripping guitar licks. I sat enraptured in a twisted sort of way.

> *I'm a rolling thunder, a pouring rain*
> *I'm comin' on like a hurricane*
> *My lightning's flashing across the sky*
> *You're only young but you're gonna die...*

By the time we passed the title track, "Back in Black," and were well-immersed in the intro of *You Shook Me All Night Long*, Dana pulled into a roughly-graveled lot, pointing to a partially-flashing, partially-lit sign, which pronounced that we were there—Ben and Todd's. Inside the store, the girls hustled to the back, while I fixated at the front on an array of pickled goods in jars. If you were freaky for pickled things, Ben and Todd had it all: pickled pickles, pickled pigs feet, pickled eggs, pickled okra...you name it. Noticing that I was dressed in a school football

.
.
.
.
.

game jersey, a large gray-headed man standing behind the counter with a pistol anchored firmly into a side holster, who must have been Ben, or Todd, asked if I played ball.

"Oh, yes sir. I've got a game tonight."

"I didn't know high schools around here played on Thursday night," he said.

"Well, they don't. I'm just in the ninth grade."

"Humppphhhh."

The girls arrived at the counter just in time, plunking two packs of Miller ponies down for purchase. Ben, or Todd, took Dana's $4.58 in exact change, placed the pony packs in brown paper bags and shoved us off. Back into the car and on our way back in the direction of school, Beth handed me a little bitty beer. I looked at the top.

"How do I get this off?" The girls howled in laughter.

"Twist it."

I took a sniff, and gagged in response. I looked ahead at Dana, and already, her beer was all but gone. Beth was half-way there. Sensing pressure to reduce the amount of liquid in my bottle, I held my breath and turned it up, pouring two or three ounces directly down the back of my throat. However, the fourth ounce got blocked by the trap door of my tongue and spewed all down the space between the bottle and my throat. My taste buds went numb, which initiated a startling reaction. As I tried to swallow, I was also throwing up. I made a gurgle noise loud enough that the girls could hear it over the music. They turned around, but fortunately I was able to purse my lips enough to hold the liquid from spraying across the interior of the purple car.

"You like it?" Dana wanted to know.

Sure, I was thinking to myself, nothing better than puke and gross beer. But that's not what I said. After choking down the gulp and other contents, I professed with watery eyes that the beer was just fine.

I managed to finish the first pony and part of one more before the girls, who sucked down seven each, dropped me off, back at the school. Welcome to the High Life, they told me, after turning down the music as we pulled up in the parking lot. As I exited the car, Dana got out, too, giving a parting hug. I noticed that her eyes did not appear to be nearly as crossed and that her thighs seemed to have thinned, but it would be several years later before I would fully understand that phenomenon. Back at school, in the locker room, I was approached by my football team's head coach, who had a snickering look on his face.

"Where have you been?"

"Uh…"

"I just saw you drive up in a purple car with two girls that I have never seen you with before. If I did not know better, I would say you have been up to no good."

"Uh…"

Thankfully, the coach walked off before I could answer and the day became just another of oddball, youthful memories. The girls and I would never spend meaningful time together again after our trip to Ben and Todd's, but I did run into them occasionally throughout the next eight years or so due to the smallness of the town in which we lived. Typically, they were together and typically, one, or both, would either have a beer in their hand or would be talking about their intentions of having a beer in their hand soon. I'm also relatively sure that, when the spirits called, Dana and her friend weren't shy to puff a magic dragon. Perhaps, they even tackled something stronger on occasion. But the little time I spent with these girls revealed to me that, for the most part, they lived for the (legal) High Life. Nothing more, nothing less.

That's the way the South was back in the day, a simple kind of place where people just reached for a cold beer if they got entangled in the web of downtroddenness and needed something to take their mind away from worries.

Not anymore.

Take, for example, the woman who was held hostage by the courthouse shooting suspect in Atlanta in 2005. She said publicly, before the media and God, that she talked the man into turning himself in by reading passages from a popular faith-based book. Sales of the hardback soared in response and people crowed. "That Ashley Smith," they said, "what a fine Christian girl she is." The devil went and knocked on her pretty stained glass door, and she answered it with a choir girl smile and unflagging faith.

Oh, troubled, fugitive black man, don't you have a purpose in your life? Won't you take a tip from my cute, smug little white self and save your pathetic, black-ass soul?

Her heroics of talking the man into turning himself into authorities before harming anyone else got her on Larry King and most all of the national talk shows, allowing her to flash a purifying grin and explain to the hardened world how she was just a sweet old Southern girl who could. As a result, Ms. Smith got a six-figure book deal, which she apparently celebrated at her favorite Georgia honky-tonk by knocking back a shooter or six of truth serum.

No longer called to be an angel, she determined after the fat book contract her purpose in life was to be a tell-all author. Never mind that she probably spells literary, L-I-T-R-A-I-R-Y, and that the last book she probably read before *A Purpose-Driven Life* was the audio version of Sue Grafton's *A is for Alibi*, which, even in audible format, was so overwhelming and difficult to finish that she couldn't bear to attempt the rest of the alphabetic book series. To her credit, Ms. Smith did not let her lack of creative experience stop her new-found purpose in life. She bared her supposedly-saved-soul right down to the nub, telling the public for the first time that in addition to discussing the book *A Purpose-Driven Life* with suspected gunman Brian Nichols, she also gave him some crystal methamphetamine from her personal stash to snort up his nose.

One can only hope that she did not do for the drug what she did for the book. Apparently, it is popular enough in the South already, threatening to drag lower and lower-middle income classes of whites into a full-fledged crisis. The government estimates that there are only around 1.5 million regular meth users in this country, but anybody who has spent much time in Kentucky, Arkansas, Tennessee or Georgia will testify that the number of users exceed that.

A 27-year-old widowed mother and working-class woman with children, Ms. Smith is the epitome of the Southern meth user. Many turn to the drug initially for its stamina and mood-altering abilities, but once on it, most have trouble leaving it alone and fall into the despair of rapid physical decline, parental neglect and poor decision-making. Never before have women been so attracted to such a lethal drug. In the South, it is causing a significant domestic problem, since many are not as lucky as Smith, who landed a lucrative book contract and a breezy makeover for having gotten a thug stoned, before preaching to him.

Take, for instance, another Georgia woman who claimed in media accounts in 2005 to have had a meth addiction for 10 years, while remaining married and raising a family the entire time. A regular, addicted user, suffering all of the most horrible consequences the drug can inflict, she claimed to have lost multiple teeth due to the damage from caustic chemicals mixed in the drug; she developed open wounds and subsequent scabs on her arms and legs and suffered profuse wrinkling of the face, yet her family supposedly didn't know about the problem.

"Notice anything different about me, honey?" she might have asked her husband, flashing a toothless smile on her haggard, worn-hard face.

"Yeah, babe, sorry...nice shirt."

And we wonder why some would turn to such a powerful drug.

Lower income women in the South tend to be more overweight and the typically have less-than-desirable jobs and a multitude of responsibilities when children are involved. Meth abusers often lose weight since food carries little interest when you're taking apart and rebuilding car engines for fun, and in the early stages of use, many report euphoria from the numbing energy. One little snort or puff of this stuff, and you feel omnipotent for 10 hours. No wonder the Atkins Diet tapered off. Who wouldn't give up chronic goat-meat breath when you can just as easily shed the pounds while experiencing chemically-induced euphoria?

There's also this alluring scenario: "Let me get this straight: You want me to work a 10-hour shift, come home, do laundry, feed the kids and then ride around on that limp little pogo stick of yours?"

Snort.

"Okay, that all sounds fine. Which one should I do first?"

Worsening the situation is the fact that anybody can learn how to make the drug, cooking together ingredients that may include lighter fluid, lithium battery strips, Drano, ammonia and concentrations of ephedrine or pseudo ephedrine. Not exactly a tantalizing recipe, like Mrs. Field's secret cookie recipe that wasn't supposed to get out, but did enough to get some people hooked. And when the drug takes lives over, bad things happen to kind-of-good people. With an incessant urge to scratch drug-induced itches, scabs are rarely left alone to heal by users. One woman I recall reading about told grotesquely about how she and other addicts would sometimes go the unimaginable step further than scratching scabs. They'd actually remove them by hand, ingesting these bodily crusts, in hopes that dispelled remnants of the drug could be orally recycled.

The act gives new meaning to the ever-present question: Do you want fries with that?

Not all meth users are as disgusting, or obvious. One young 20-something-year-old girl I know, who attended a Southeastern Conference school for two years and who comes from a nice, middle-class family, told me of a friend handing her a pipe filled with a funny-smelling, wispy drug.

"Smoke this," she was told.

And she did, soaring into the most hyper-confident and seemingly aware state she said a human can imagine. Energetic and more sexually alert from the super-sized stimulant dose, she reported having tried it several more times before recognizing its highly seductive, and therefore addicting, powers. A cold beer in comparison with meth, she said, was like comparing Bac-Os to a freshly-fried slab of premium bacon; one is just a pretender.

The young girl was among the rare meth victims able to turn away. Most aren't so fortunate, and the victims who appear to be suffering the most are women, many with jobs and children at home. If they are overworked, underappreciated, and feeling generally hopeless in life, meth seems like a reasonable-enough hobby.

-
-
-
-
-

No needlepoint for this girl, just give her a hit of crank to pass the time.

The problem is that, the drug's crippling effects are creating a social emergency as many women spend their days tweaking, instead of nurturing. They are giving birth to a new generation of Southern children who will recall, when asked about their mother years from now, that she never really did much of anything, other than occasionally stand over a hot stove, slaving. It never smelled like much, but, jeez, she sure did get excited when it was done.

Chapter Five

.
.
.
.
.
.

Santa vs. Satan

THE SMELL OF A SUMMER'S dust burning from home heating units at first ignition and the merciful removal of a last, slightly-red runt tomato from a shriveled and dying vine can only mean one thing each year in the South: my least favorite calendar event of the year is near. I'm not exactly sure at what point in life my disdain for Halloween took hold, but I do know that since I was old enough to get caramel and nougat stuck in my teeth, I have bristled at the abundance of plastic, candy, slight mayhem and general cheapness that emanates from this kiddie freak show.

It is true that years ago, when my children were small, I gained pleasant memories from the imagination and innocence inspired by their donning of costume. I will also admit to the brief but satisfactory enjoyment of attending one or two adult masquerade parties along the way. But for the most part, I find myself hoping the pseudo-holiday will quickly pass. It is an odd objection, I know, particularly since so many residents of Dixie are so enamored with spookiness, celebrating from Tunica, Mississippi to Gadsden, Alabama, with giant, inflatable witches and crooked-teeth jack-o-lanterns (how else would we carve pumpkins when most of us haven't ever seen a full set of straight teeth?), drapes of fake spider webs on porches and in trees and mounds of candy in bowls throughout the house.

While I'm looking forward to the first day of November, when the remnants of Halloween are swept away in anticipation of a more gracious, thankful event, others are anticipating the big day, buying out every Wal-Mart shelf filled with a hodgepodge of kitschy orange and black decorations. The plastic, talking witch that hangs on the wall is not enough; they need candy dispensers in the shape of a skull, and fake blood and shrieking sounds and lots and lots of little, tiny candy bars.

On the big day, children are called to momentarily become someone, or something, from their wildest imagination. Grownups, on the other hand, are called to simply embrace the zaniness of it all, laughing and smiling and praising oodles of costumed young ones, dressed up as everything from ghostly figures to contemporary characters. Next, they are ushered into the streets, which they "must never play on at night for every other day of the year," and told to query neighbors to see whether they will offer a treat, or suffer at the hands of a cruel trick. Always, they defer to the treat. Unless, of course, they have none; then, they just turn out the lights, hoping the sugar-high vagabonds will quietly go away.

That's not how Halloween started out, however. The event traces back to the ancient religion of the Celtics, who believed that forces keeping evil spirits away from the living became very weak during the peak of fall, allowing souls of the dead to move more freely among the living. Some believed the free-running spirits-of-the-dead returned to their original haunts, creating havoc for all. Treats were offered to appease them, and villagers tried to blend in among the prospective marauders by dressing up as vile and demonic beings rather than being identified as vulnerable humans.

Perhaps more than anything, Halloween's origin is what makes it such a strange and confusing event in the South. The region known as the Bible Belt has emerged in the 21st century as the most prolific buyer of specialty goods related to the evil spirit-rooted celebration, from the world's largest retailer. It is neither the Neurotic North nor the Wild West which sharply boosts retail sales during the last week of October; it is the conservative, witchcraft-is-the-devil's-brew South, fueling the ever-growing business that's rooted in the centuries-old pagan practice. Going all out for Easter, I can understand, although the fixation on a giant, leaping rabbit and its faux eggs isn't much more comforting. At least the colors are softer, with muted pastels, and little children are dressed as angels, not devils.

Halloween, I've just never been able to put my arms around it for a hug, and it's not just the cheapness, the gaudy colors or the strangeness of celebration that leave me puzzled. With all the advances made in spooky paraphernalia, masquerades have not exactly kept up with the go-go times. For generations, people trying to be scary have dressed in varying costumes, from the grim reaper to the evil witch to the all-time favorite skeleton. One hundred years ago, I could maybe understand how passing a grim reaper or a goblin on Halloween night, in, say, Pikesville, Kentucky, might have freaked a person out. But now, they're as harmless as a little Buzz Lightyear bop bop bopping along. Nowadays, I walk down the street on Halloween night, pass a grim reaper, and keep on going, fearlessly. It's like watching *Friday the 13th* for the 13th time—far too predictable, unable to stir up detectable fright. It has gotten so bad, that even the once-dreaded evil witch has a hard time of getting any reaction out of me. When she comes a-knocking on my door, I'm hardly amused, much less terrified.

"Oh, it's you again."

Yawn.

"Go on. Cast a spell…whatever. Hit me with your best shot."

If someone wants to visit my Tennessee home and deliver a scare, it's going to take a bit more creativity than these out-of-date, antiquated spooks. Take the cigarette, for example. That sultry, seductive stick has been killing people, especially Southerners, by the thousands for decades. It got so bad that, a few years ago, a private practice lawyer named Dickie Scruggs had to join up with some Southern states, like Mississippi, and sue the big cigarette manufacturing companies for damages. Of course, after a settlement worth billions and reams of public education later, Southerners are still smoking, and dying. On the other hand, I don't recall a single report of a death attributed to a grim reaper. That's why if a walking, three-and-a-half-foot cigarette knocks on my door, asking for candy, I'm going to quiver, dish out the goods, then duck and run for the fire extinguisher.

"Trick or treat, you say? Here, no tricks, just take it all…the whole basket. It's yours, just please, go away."

Spooks could even stand to get regionally creative, specifically catering to fears according to each zip code. In Auburn, Alabama, a Bear Bryant mask and hounds tooth hat would likely send shivers up the neighbor's spines, just as a ghoul posing as a weatherman holding a hurricane warning sign would probably do the same along the Mississippi Gulf Coast. In east Tennessee, a Steve Spurrier visor and clipboard would do the trick, while in Memphis, posing as a white man in a cop uniform will send them running. A bit far-fetched, perhaps, but, anything is better than what we currently have, which is a lame attempt at being scary that ends up celebrating things garish, not ghouls.

Halloween, however, has nothing on the conflicting approach some Southerners are taking in regard to Christmas. Leading the charge in 2005 to boycott big-box retailers like Wal-Mart and Target for greeting customers with "Happy Holidays" signs were Baptists from Tupelo, Mississippi to Timmonsville, South Carolina. The general accusation is that by using generic, non-theological holiday greetings, retailers were removing the Christ- from the -mas of Christmas. Never mind that George W. Bush, the President of the United States, elected on the backbone strength of conservative, Southern states, sent out greeting cards wishing supporters "Happy Holidays." Shopping boycotts were urged and corporate smear campaigns launched, urging people to unite and protect their sacred celebration. One group even went so far as to rhetorically ask potential purchasers, "Where would Jesus shop?"

In my hometown, the answer probably wouldn't be one store versus another, but along the banks of the Tennessee River. I'm certain, though, Jesus would get far enough downstream that the government's tainted fish warning signs would be out of sight. No sense gathering fish to multiply if they are poisoned with PCBs and too hazardous to consume. But, as for the so-called non-Christian conforming stores, I can't imagine he would care much, since shopping in December in large quantity is really more of an economic function than a celebration of his birth. How shoppers are being greeted during the holiday sales season would likely not matter nearly as much as the pay rate and the quantity and quality of benefits being received annually by hourly employees of these companies.

"Happy holidays, sir," the greeter might say.

"Oh, thank you, and bless you, my lady. Let me ask you, how much are you earning in wages for standing by this cold door and warming the hearts of entering patrons all day long?

"What? Five dollars and seventy five cents an hour, with no benefits? Why, a loaf of bread costs, what, three dollars? That's blasphemy, I tell you."

:

More importantly, though, nothing would likely matter nearly as much as the vain and contradictory approach many Christians take to Christmas, practicing and fostering myths, if not disillusionment, with traditions as cemented as a turkey on a Thanksgiving table. Take Santa Claus, for example. I have not yet read the entire Bible, but even though I've found no references in it to the pudgy man in the red suit, I'm expecting him to eventually show up mysteriously at the end, a la a surprising John Grisham suspense plot.

I can see it unfolding now. It will not be Christ who gets tied to a cross and brutally tortured, as I have heard. Rather, the man nailed to the planks through his hands and feet and hoisted high above the ground to die will be the once-Jolly Old St. Nick himself.

Your day has come, fat man.

The thought makes me shudder, images of blood running down from his thorn-wounded crown and across those tiny, rosy-red cheeks before settling on and staining his fluffy white beard; sounds of his template "ho, ho, ho" turning to skin-crawling cries of deathly anguish; and his bowl-full-of-jelly belly quivering in devastating pain.

"Ho, ho, ho, ho, ho…ho, ho, ho…ahhh, ahhhh, aaaaaaahhhhhhhh!"

What else explains the passion and propagation so many

Christians feel for this man during what is to be their most sacred celebration of the year, if he does not appear in the pages among Peter, Paul and Mary? A real crowd favorite to this day, men masquerading in the image of Santa Claus draw lines of people with impressionable young children in tow in stores and in shopping malls. If that's not enough, for years and years, statuesque figures of his likeness have been prominently displayed during the holidays, both inside of individual houses and out. When letter inquiries of want are addressed during the season, deference is given not to a man known as Jesus, but to a man known as Claus.

What do you want for Christmas? People rarely respond with this: a foot massager, a new titanium driver and ever-lasting life. It is He who is said to provide forgiveness, but it is he who is said to deliver the goods, like computers, video games, dolls and cellular telephones. But in regard to Mr. Claus, this is a farce. Such items, we know, come from a store, having more to do with who has money than which little boys and girls have been good or bad. Yet even in complete awareness of this fact, many Southern Christians still seem to spend more of their time during the season in pursuit of the fantasy, embracing the happiest of holidays over the actual miracle of Christmas.

"What do you want from Santa, dear? A new bike, you say? Well, be a good little girl for Santa and that may just

·
·
·
·
·

well happen. Now, put that new dress on and let's hurry up and go, or, you'll be late for Sunday School."

At church, the parents gather in one room, sharing outrage with one another, over coffee and doughnuts, that suddenly, greedy retailers are no longer operating in the proper spirit of the season by greeting shoppers with "Happy Holidays." In response, they collectively decide to boycott. Then, pleased at their action, they gather up their children and smugly drive home. Turning in the driveway, they notice the sunshine glistening off of the large, plastic Santa Claus, anchored in the yard next to an accompanying sleigh and eight reindeer. Their eyes glisten, even moisten perhaps, as they experience full emotions from the glee and beauty of the Christmas season before them.

Chapter Six

．
．
．
．
．
．

Sweet Corn–How Sweet It Is

THERE ARE SOME PREFERENTIAL TASTES held closely by Southerners that no amount of modern culture can overcome. No matter how much time one spends reading the "Dining Out" section of *The New York Times*, with stories about such trendy American eateries as Manhattan's BLT Steak or esoteric foods such as tapas or menu appetizers like duck egg with tuna bottarga, the Southerner inevitably migrates back to the same regional foods and flavors of his and her homeland. Admittedly, these perusers of "Dining Out" are at the same time avid readers of *Racer Magazine*, who could also be considered chain buffet snobs with a lifelong affection for Dolly Madison Zingers.

Back-country favorites like rib tips, slow-cooked brisket,

fried bologna sandwiches, and even potted meat spread haphazardly over crackers are included into this group of beloved treats, but it's the traditional and fresh fruits of labor, and the season, that directly touch the heart and truly tantalize the palates of almost every child of the South. Yes, even to this day. From black-eyed peas (doused after cooking with ketchup or chow-chow, of course), okra, cantaloupe, watermelon, peaches, new potatoes, cabbage, tomatoes—especially tomatoes—corn, and squash; fresh produce is the ultimate conquest. Often, such treasures are grown in the gardens of friends and neighbors and passed along like seeds of a coveted, endangered flower. But since there is never enough to go around, most have to turn to roadside produce stands, *presumably* run by local gardeners and farmers, to get their stock.

Memories from my earliest days always drift back to my mother tossing me into the back of the family Ford wagon for a trip to the farmer's market, where locals with harvested crops gathered at a roadside stand in unison to sell everything from snap peas to zucchinis. Most were dressed, predictably, in overalls and plaid shirts. They looked, and smelled, like they had not bathed in a few days, with dirt under fingernails and slight stench drifting in the breeze. But they had the goods; man, did they ever have the fresh goods.

"There here 'maters, they are the best I've ever growed."

(Taking out a pocket knife, the farmer slices a bite from a large, perfectly round, red Big Boy variety).

"Try dis un, boy."

Chew, chew: gulp.

"See what I mean? Good, ain't it?"

The memory, as well as the flavors, have kept me stopping at one out of every four produce stands I've passed along on Southern roads ever since. Through the years, I have purchased some of the best ears of corn and cantaloupes and tomatoes a person could find. Ever since the turn of the century, however, I began to notice an alarming trend—more often than not, purchased produce was of poor quality rather than good. Worried that a good thing might be ending, I made particular effort last summer to stop at even more roadside stands.

During weeks of travel by car to points near and far in the Deep South, the sight of a sign promising fresh produce or a man standing beside a truck with an open tailgate was a sign to whip the car over in a hairpin. It was an occasion calling for the blatant disregard of traffic laws, Newton's laws, and the odd 18-wheeler coming from the opposite direction. This, after all, was the innate desire to eat well, prove that a great tradition was not dying, and reward hard workers of the field. But the patronage left me only with a burning question.

-
-
-
-
-
-

What has happened to the integrity of the roadside produce stand in the 21st century south?

As nice and well-intentioned as the people may have been that I encountered in states including Arkansas, Georgia, Alabama, Mississippi, Tennessee and Florida, they opened my eyes to the harsh reality: Most of these people don't grow the stuff themselves anymore. Idealistically, I still had envisioned the young boy and his overall-wearing father from whom I bought a bagful of tomatoes and a cantaloupe outside Montgomery, Ala., taking to the field together the first day in May that school was out. Pa and boy, I imagined, got up early, plowing the dirt and sowing seed together. Pa and boy, I imagined, got up early the next day and the days after that, ignoring the rising temperature and humidity to water, weed and stake.

This is the way it is done, son. This is the value of land, son. This is why water is precious, son. This is the value of work, son. This is how you become a man, son.

I did not realize you were so strong, Pa. I did not realize how much you loved the land, Pa. I did not understand the circle of life, Pa. I love you so much, Pa.

At first glance, I had come to the right place. It was just early June, but the tomatoes displayed on a shoddy, unpainted wooden table set up less than 10 yards from the opened bed of a 1970s model Ford pickup, completely filled with cantaloupes and watermelons, were large, round and red, excellent in appearance even for South Alabama with the Fourth of July still weeks away.

"You guys did great," I said, while fondling their fruit.

"Yep," responded the large, older man wearing overalls, who followed his words with a brown stream of tobacco that splattered on the dry, dusty ground.

I asked for a bag and was given a plastic one labeled with the logo from Kroger, as in the grocery store, Kroger. Nevertheless, I filled the bag until it could hold no more, handing it to the boy. He weighed them on a small scale.

"That'll be $11," he said in a high-pitched voice.

Satisfied that I had obtained quality tomatoes grown by a father-son team, I gloated over them the rest of the way home, fantasizing about cutting into one and eating it later.

"I'm going to eat the fattest tomato sandwich you've ever seen," I said. "No, I'm going to eat two of the fattest tomato sandwiches you've ever seen."

Minutes after returning home, I removed the large tomato from the bag, washed them off, and removed the stub of a stem with a knife. I then proceeded to slice it into one-inch slabs, only to find that, once again, I had been taken. The tomato's skin was tough and the inside was mealy. It had obviously been picked while still green,

•
•
•
•
•

weeks before from some place more decidedly un-Southern, like California, or Mexico, if not from the inside of a greenhouse. Talk about dashing a dream, from watering at the mouth to foaming at the mouth and the imposter vegetables were sent hurtling to the trash, along with the rosy pictures in my mind.

How it really happened, I now had it figured, was that boy slept past noon that first day after school, a comfortable event that was repeated over and over again throughout a lazy summer. Sometime around midmorning, Pa slid into his extended cab pickup, cranked the air conditioner up to maximum delivery, and drove to some wholesale shop.

"Let's see," he probably said. "I'll take them, some of them and a box of them over there."

Pa was probably home by two in the afternoon, and when the sleepy-headed boy finally cut off the video game, they each slipped on overalls, got into the truck, drove down the road a bit, pulled over to a good spot, and went to work, appealing to the raw emotions of early-summer travelers.

"Hey, boy, look…here comes another sucker, right there."

Always the optimist, I stopped at another stand the very next week on another road trip, trying yet again to obtain homegrown, fresh produce. Somewhere near the

Gulf of Mexico, around Mobile, I think, I remembered to ask the roadside proprietor the origin of his fine-looking fruit. It was from Tennessee, he said, revealing a refreshing honesty.

"Bradley County, I think."

"Gee," I told him. "That's just 25 minutes from my house. Had I known, I could have brought a load on down, saving a trip."

Still not willing to give in, my quest for roadside produce excellence continued that week after that fateful stop. I was traveling east, having just crossed the Mississippi River, and coasting along the Arkansas flatlands, the nearest town being a tiny crossroads named Marvel, which was 20 minutes in my rearview mirror. Suddenly, I came up on a man standing by a truck, which was surrounded with tables covered in produce. He was set up at an intersection stop in the road. Pulling in for a look-see, I recognized he was just selling one thing—peaches. Considering that an exceedingly fresh, Southern-grown peach constitutes nirvana to me, I wanted to give this man every chance to make a sale. If these peaches came from his trees, I would buy bushels full.

"They are from Cabot," he said. "Best you'll find."

Cabot was near enough, but not so for him to be set up from the back of his truck and selling near Marvel.

They did look good and smelled good, I had to admit. And growing peaches is much harder than growing tomatoes and melons, so, fair enough. The stop apparently got better, however, when a skinny, older, overall-wearing man stepped in from the right, placing on a table he had just set up, a handwritten sign for me to see.

"Sweet Corn—How Sweet It Is."

Finally, some real local produce to gnaw on.

"How you like that?" the man said, referring to his sloppy, but catchy sign. "Sounds like Jackie Gleason, don't it?"

"Sure it does," I responded. "Hey, this is just what I've been looking for. For almost a month, I've been driving all over the South, stopping at every roadside produce stand I've seen in search of some fresh, homegrown goods. Give me a bag full. No, give me two bags full."

"You see," the man said, "that there is the problem. This corn is so good, we done sold out. I just put this sign up here to make you aware."

"That's too bad."

"Well," he said, "Tell you what. If you're passing back through tomorrow morning, stop by. But make sure it's after 10. It takes me at least two hours to drive up to Batesville and buy some more."

Chapter Seven

•
•
•
•
•
•

There's No Room for the Mexicans

As a child in Mississippi who began public school as a first grade student in 1971, I was part of what should have been a post-integration progress, fostering harmony, understanding and common ground between blacks and whites. Starting with a clean mental slate as youthful innocents, largely unaware of the baggage which preceded us, including murder, mayhem and considerable misunderstanding, my generation could've been bestowed with the tools and materials needed to build a bridge, one that would that would both link and bind the previously isolated worlds of Southern blacks and whites.

From my perspective, everything started out just fine. Our class was split almost exactly down even racial lines;

•
•
•
•
•

we were the picture-perfect poster of what American education was supposed to look like—children from different
racial and economic backgrounds learning together, playing together and growing together. My favorite friend
was a boy nicknamed Ferret, presumably because he was
small, skinny and slinky. I rarely did or said anything that
I thought was humorous without looking at Ferret to see
if he was laughing. In return, he followed me wherever I
went, on the playground, in the lunchroom, to the bathroom—everywhere. At Valentine's, we exchanged cards. I
opened mine, finding the exact same inscription that I had
written in his, "best friend."

In the summer after school, we never saw each other,
though, in reality, we probably lived not more than three
miles from one another. But I remember vividly the first
day of second grade, walking into my new homeroom class,
seeing Ferret seated at a corner desk, smiling broadly. We
talked so much during the first week of class the teacher
had to split us up. It didn't hamper our friendship, though.
Neither did the third, fourth or fifth grade, years that fate,
or homeroom teachers, did not place us in the same class-
room. On the playground, we met and talked, laughing,
chasing girls, playing touch football. You name it, we did
it, happily; ebony and ivory, together in perfect harmony.

One day in the lunchroom when we were fifth graders,

Ferret invited me to spend the night at his house on an upcoming Friday. He would have to ask his mother, of course. Then, I could ask mine. The next day, however, he shyly reported back to me that his mother had not simply said no, but said hell no, as in, ain't no honky ass white boy spending the night in my house. Surprised, but accepting the fact, I reported to my mother later the same night what had transpired at school. Understanding that I would not, in fact, be spending the night with Ferret, a relieved look spread over her face.

It was probably just as well since I later found out he lived in a small apartment in the projects and, although his father was never there and his mother rarely was, seeing that she worked two jobs, he still had to make do with five older brothers and sisters. Besides, as we moved into junior high and high school, our differences became more apparent, and, even though we remained friends, the common ground on which we previously stood had shifted, considerably. By the tenth grade, our more infrequent conversations consisted mostly of his seeking, or sharing, facts about sex or the female anatomy. I recall, for instance, him asking details about making out with white girls. When I told him about tongue-kisses and soft breasts, he was generally bored, wanting, instead, to get right down to what mattered most, the vagina.

•
•
•
•
•

Did a white girl's look different than a black girl's?

After reporting that I had encountered neither, and therefore, could offer no comparison, Ferret told me he would do some research and let me know. And sure enough, just when I thought I would not speak to my friend again, he would show up from around a corner, or at my car in the parking lot, or in the boy's bathroom at school, sharing his less-than-scientific findings. On one particular mid-afternoon at school, he shoved me into a locker in the hall as an excited, friendly gesture. I knew that he felt he had made some highly classified finding. This was confirmed when he held two fingers up just beneath my nose, giving the command, "smell." Only because I *had* to breathe did I inhale. The initial whiff was bad enough, but it registered considerably worse after he reported that, a few minutes before, he was visiting with a sizeable girl named Felicia.

"I think I'm going to be sick," I told him.

"You a white boy," Ferret said.

"That's right. What's your point?"

"I would think you wanna smell a black girl."

That's where he was wrong, racial reasons notwithstanding.

Soon enough, Ferret and I went separate ways, taking the friendship and lessons learned from one another along as fond memories. We did not know it, of course, but hindsight reveals that we were the centerpiece for an attempted movement in this country, to bring whites and blacks together under one roof to learn with equal opportunity. We were poster children perhaps, for what the integrated South was supposed to look like, but I am sorry to say that some 25 years later, not much progress has been made from that point. To be sure, there is co-mingling among blacks and whites living below the Mason-Dixon Line, both in the workplace, schools, and even in some neighborhoods, but for the most part, the south is still a great racial divide. Most public schools are still greatly imbalanced in racial percentages, some 35 years after integration, since address, i.e. economics, dictates which schools students attend and the great busing experiment did not work. Racial division grows even greater outside of classrooms, with most people living in neighborhoods and worshipping in churches that are mostly segregated not by law, but by culture, the preferences of blacks and whites who, apparently, prefer being surrounded by people of their own race when praying, or laying down to sleep. In Memphis, for instance a city where minorities are the majority, some all-white, affluent neighborhoods exist where affluent blacks would never consider buying a home, not because they fear being tarred and feathered, but because they don't want to live among a bunch of stuffy, lily whites.

Choice of neighborhood does not sum up the south's great racial divide in the 21st century south as well as what occurs in churches from Texas to North Carolina on Sunday mornings. Why blacks and whites who profess to worship the same God and often belong to the same denomination have no interest in sitting together on the same pews has always boggled my Mississippi-molded mind. Most metropolitan cities, like Atlanta, Chattanooga and Memphis, have one or two churches that promote bi-racial worship, but Sunday morning drive-bys in most cities and towns in the heart of Dixie quickly reveal that the people going in and coming out are either all black, or all white. It is all ebony and ivory, worshiping as far away from each other as possible in complete disharmony...

The reasons for this great divide are multiple, beginning with the simple fact that for most white people, church is a place for repentance that is to be carried out as stiffly and stoically and traditionally as possible. The service should last X minutes, and not a second longer. Shorter is fine, of course. The music should consist of the same songs sung 100 years ago, and 100 years before that, and the preacher shouldn't show more emotion than a lightly starched Polo shirt.

Church for most black people, on the other hand, involves a mutating service that grows and flows like an

amoeba, with no boundaries and an ever-changing struc-
ture. Based more on emotion of the moment than rituals
of the past, they are the antithesis of stuffy and uninspir-
ing, but substance is often left to the eye of the beholder. I
went to a black church service for the first time a couple of
years ago, and, even though I frequently feel my skin crawling on Sunday mornings at the home church when I look
around and find myself surrounded by praising parishio-
ners who look like they all bathed in Martha White flower
before arriving at the sanctuary, I had a hard time adjusting to the overall hustle and flow of the black church. For
starters, when my watch passed high noon and the minute
hand kept going and going along with the preacher, who
didn't seem to care that the worship hour had ended and
the lunch hour had begun, I started to panic that every
chicken leg in town would already be sold and that I would
collapse from starvation before the day was done.

Dear Lord, I prayed, let me eat.

Once the preacher finally ended his message just before
one, I was still breathing, but not exactly thinking clearly.
I imagined myself immersed in a giant vat of mashed potatoes and green beans and had a vision of an angel above
pouring iced tea into my mouth. I thought this was a
divine sign that the service was over, but when the choir
started singing praise hymns and most of the congregation

except for me formed a line for their turn at testimonial solo, I realized that, while my heart was in the right place in regard to a black church, my stomach clearly was not. Like low-carbohydrate bread or sugar free ice cream, I tried it once, and it was okay, but I never went back.

The division of whites and blacks on Sunday mornings is not the only sign that the two races could not exist farther apart. Time after time, in elections from Clarksville, Tennessee to Montgomery, Alabama, the majority of blacks and whites vote completely opposite of one another at the polls. Take Memphis, again, as a prime example. The only time a white candidate can get elected there is from a gerrymandered district line, just as the reverse is true in many mostly-white communities. Otherwise, a black will get the popular vote every time just as a white gets the popular vote every time in say, Germantown, a white-flight suburb of the city. It does not matter if the candidates have a less-than-sterling reputation, with secret families sprinkled throughout the state and a criminal record. In Memphis, if the candidate is black and the opponent is white, they are getting into office.

I'm not sure, in fact, why black candidates in the area even bother to campaign with a serious tone, talking about issues and what-not. They would probably best be served by exposing their blackness to the highest degree, as not to lose a single vote to someone who might have trouble distinguishing between light brown and dark white. Instead of a campaign platform, the candidate could get a hat and put it on crooked. He could get some big gaudy chains and wrap them around his neck. In photo shoots, he could grab his crotch and slump his shoulders, making himself look as black as a black stereotype can be, removing any and all potential confusion from the voters. And if there is any doubt still, he could rap his own campaign song to the beat of the once-popular hick hop single *(I Play) Chicken with the Train*: "I don't know crap, but I'm blackety-black, together let's jump the track, a like that…"

And it's not one bit different for whites, who vote strictly down racial lines in cities and towns across the South, making it all but impossible for a talented minority to emerge. If two whites are running against each other, the issues *might* come into play, but if a white is running against black, forget it: the majority of votes are going to honky, even if he or she is a complete and utter fool. And the oddest thing is, if a white is running against a black, he or she doesn't even try to hide the fact when campaigning to fellow whites that a vote for someone of the opposite race would be considered a crime against (segregated) humanity.

"You know," it has been said, "we don't want *them* to get too much power."

Them, them, them. The candidates should just make it easy for voters, stand outside polling stations with signs that say something along the lines of, "Don't Forget, Blacken in a Spot for Whitey."

Some of the racial division, I understand. After all, it was not much more than a century-and-a-half ago that whites in the South owned black slaves. Not only would they not apologize for the indiscretion, they were willing to go to war and die over it. Time does heal all wounds, eventually, but another century may have to pass before the infraction is reconciled.

The oppression and general rejection given to blacks by most whites is a bit harder to understand. What have they done to us, anyway? What's more, many whites seem to love qualities of the same blackness they shun. Just go on a Saturday night to a place like, say, Interstate Barbecue in Memphis, a black-owned business located in the black heart of the city. Interstate's ribs are made by the brothers, for the brothers, yet the line waiting for takeout orders will be three-quarters white. And what about a couple of years ago, when the rapper Nelly had a breakthrough, chart-topping CD? It was not three million brothers buying the tunes, but a bunch of middle-aged white men sending it to multi-platinum status. So many were riding around in cars, speakers blasting, them singing, "it's getting hot in here so take off all your clothes," you would think they'd been born black and steadily their skin had paled since birth.

But they have never been part of the black race, and some openly display a racial callousness, if not worse. Just last year, actions in the tiny town of Trenton, Georgia had many asking the decades-old question, Is it heritage or hate? Located less than 30 miles outside of Chattanooga in the western valley of Lookout Mountain, Trenton is a town of less than 2,000 residents, 98 percent of which are white, none of which are black. In a straw poll vote conducted one fall day in 2005 by Mayor Anthony Emanuel, 278 residents out of 373 responders said they wanted to keep flying the city flag that prominently incorporates the Confederate battle emblem. The mayor had taken the city flag down, hoping nobody would care, or notice. But when many citizens revolted, suggesting the Confederate battle emblem was such a part of their heritage that it should remain as part of the city flag, he put the issue to a vote. The majority ruled.

With the stars and bars firmly back in place, odds are high that Trenton's demographic data is not going to change for some time. One can only imagine thoughts that might go through the minds of an African America couple relocating to the Chattanooga metropolitan area, looking for a place to live. They find an affordable house in a decent

-
-
-
-
-

neighborhood in Trenton. Then, they see the flag flying at city hall.

"Honey, I'm sure it really is a nice place (for minorities)," one might say. "What do symbols mean, anyway?"

"Perhaps you are right, but just to be safe, Dear, I would rather live over in Rossville."

And that's the point, isn't it?

For some whites, the display of the Confederate battle flag is an attempt to honor their ancestral past, homage to time, people and a region in which pride was arguably more at stake than rights. For just about all blacks, however, the display of the emblem in the 21st century, in a non-historical manner, is a personal affront, an in-your-face reminder of oppression, bigotry and supremacy. Like the skull and cross bones, it is a symbol of poison. Sure, you say there is fruit punch in that bottle, but I see the sign, and I'm not drinking it.

The argument that citizens made in Trenton to keep the flag has been made in the South before. For instance, fans numbering in the thousands used to wave miniature Confederate flags mounted on sticks at University of Mississippi football games, convinced it was just a show of support for the football team, not a racially-charged display. Progressive university administration asked fans beginning in the late 1980s to keep the flags out, ultimately going so far as to ban the wooden waving sticks from the stadium. Some people cried foul, arguing their rights were being violated and that Southern heritage was being trampled. At the time, the university was in a so-so state, lagging in enrollment and fund-raising. It was a collection of regional recognition and national shame. Today, however, with most of the tarnishing images quietly swept out of the way, the university is flourishing with burgeoning enrollment, record fund-raising and an image in all corners of the country as an up-and-coming public university to be reckoned with.

A similar story can be told in regard to the University of Georgia. Until 1971, its Dixie Redcoat Marching Band played "Dixie," that tear-jerking song of the old South. Then the timely decision was made to drop it from the play list, and even the word "Dixie" was expelled from the school band's official name. Wavers of the Confederate flag at games quickly dwindled in unison. What has happened at Georgia since then is nothing short of remarkable. With more than 30,000 students, it is perched among the nation's elite state universities with a broad and diverse student body that as a whole excels academically.

It is true that Georgia, as Mississippi, has benefited greatly from other factors that have fueled positive growth, like advanced giving and significantly more scholarship dollars available to attract top students. One can't help but wonder, though, if these institutions had clung steadfastly to the preservation of so-called heritage, would the transformations have ever taken place? Trenton, of course, is just a tiny municipality, having little in common with large, state institutions, but the straw votes cast showed many care little about the feelings of blacks. And, if I had to bet, it would be that the feeling is mutual.

It is a wonder, then, why the Mexicans are moving so fast into the region. I know there are better paying jobs than they can find back home, but if blacks and whites have not figured out how to thrive and grow together more than 35 years after integration, then the Mexicans can't assume there will be a welcoming environment waiting for them. Still, they keep coming and coming, causing Guinness to constantly update its book, adjusting the world record for the number of people squeezed into a van. They are some of my very favorite people, generally possessing jovial personalities and a no-fear work attitude, which is more than can be said for many blacks and whites in the South. But I will admit that it does seem at times that they are living as if on an extended work vacation where nothing needs to be taken too seriously. Take, for instance, one 14-year-old boy I know. In just his second year in the United States, he speaks fluent Spanish, yet is flunking first-year Spanish at the American public school he attends.

"Hola, Professora. Me llamo Ricki."

"But wait, son. You are not Ricki. You are Javier. Please try that again."

When asked about this, the boy just laughs, as do his parents. It is funny to them, the kid fresh from Mexico flunking Spanish. Of course, he is flunking all of his courses—English, Spanish, Math, and Science. Perhaps, though, they don't worry so much, figuring that as long as the blacks and whites don't want to clean house, work construction or man the assembly line at the chicken-cleaning factory, there will always be jobs to be had.

Probably, they are right, but once more get ambitious, deciding, for instance, to gain citizenry and run for public office, or worse, deciding to explore the benefits of attending a nearby white or black church, the carefree highway they have been following to all points throughout the South will inevitably meet some serious roadblocks.

Chapter Eight

•
•
•
•
•
•

Poor Ass White Trash Beggars

DURING A RECENT ROUTINE CONVENIENCE store stop last year, I had the disturbing realization that the lower-middle class white southerner is desperately in trouble and literally begging for help. It came to me as a gas pump scenario that plays itself out all too frequently these days unfolded near Cleveland, Tennessee, just off Interstate 75. Standing outside of the car while gas flowed into the tank one over-priced gallon after another, a middle-aged man driving a small pickup pulled up beside.

"My wife and I are driving to the hospital to see our daughter who just had a baby and I forgot my wallet at home," the man said. "Could you spare some money for gas?"

• • • • •

The man looked like he had not slept in days, and probably had not. They were not too shabbily dressed, which was surprising considering physical appearances, and, therefore, did not have the look of extreme, lifelong poverty. But, it was obvious that hard times of some serious sort had hit. Suspecting substance abuse as the culprit, I rejected their plea for funds.

Sorry, can't help…I've got my own gas to pay for. Besides, alligator skin is no longer en vogue. You'll have to put your roughed-up selves in front of someone else if you expect a brother to spare a dime. There's no better time to determine the credibility of a beggar than after a rejection and I was not disappointed nor surprised when, in response to my cold-hearted rejection, rumple stiltskin and his bride retreated to their 1970s-style Nissan mini truck, slamming both doors, just before the man hit the gas peddle with a quick "kiss my ass you stingy bastard" thump, speeding off from a cold start the best way a four-cylinder vehicle can.

At roughly 200 yards away, with the vehicle not running at more than 20 miles per house, I saw the man make a sharp turn back toward the convenience store before stopping behind an adjacent building for apparent hiding. The truck looked much like my cat does when he's stalking prey, believing he's hidden behind a door frame, while preparing to pounce on my forward-pointing, slightly jiggling feet, but in reality is showing 30 percent, or more, of his cocked and coiled felineness.

You sly cat, I see you.

There, the man and his wife found partial shelter from my sight, while maintaining their view of the gas pumps. Another potential victim to solicit would arrive soon enough. I rolled my eyes for effect to nobody but myself, initially passing the begging off for its commonality. A similar incident happened to me the week before, and the week before that, and probably, the week before that. A white southerner, seeming to have economic standing above lower class, proclaims to be down on their luck and openly and unashamedly begs for money.

Then, the realization struck: It has not always been this way.

For the first three-quarters of my life, the only open begging I encountered on a regular basis was in the heart of metropolitan areas like New Orleans and Atlanta. Typically, this came from the lowest of low in standing on the economic class ladder—homeless, unemployed beggars seeking 50 cents or one dollar.

Outside of that, I have spent significant time in some of the South's poorest areas and communities, from Tunica, Mississippi's renowned Sugar Ditch to back roads of Alabama. Some were filled by poor whites; others by poor blacks. Never, though, do I recall being stopped on the street and asked for money from my wallet. Most of these people never had much in the way of material possession and they certainly did not expect me or anyone else to give it to them. Now, situated in a class one full rung up the economic ladder, lower-middle income whites are stooping in droves to conjure up stories in an effort to have dollars handed to them at gas stations, in grocery store parking lots and on suburban streets.

Brother, can you spare a 10-spot? My wife is sick and I done lost my wallet. I need to take my wife to the doctor.

Without question, a leading culprit of this growing socio-economic problem is growing use of illegal crystal methamphetamine in the white, rural South. The addictive drug is sucking the lifeblood out of previously productive workers and threatening to erode family, as well as moral, fiber. But there are more contributors to this problem than the highly-publicized drug epidemic. For starters, the explosion of state-sponsored gambling initiatives in the South in the past 15 years has probably caused more damage than any social worker can document. The demographic that gambles the most or buys the most lottery tickets, for instance, is wage earners without college degrees—also known as the lower-middle or working class.

Years of having money siphoned off of household

incomes by casinos and lotteries that are now abundant in the South are likely taking a toll. Sure, Mississippi has reaped millions for education since casinos were legalized in the early 1990s, and sure, thousands of Georgia residents have gotten a free education due to the purchase of lottery tickets, but at what price?

Adding insult to this already severe personal injury is the fact that as the South and much of the rest of the nation makes its less-than-beautiful metamorphosis from industry jobs to service, the lower-middle class is getting left even further behind. With the erosion of employee benefits and wages comes the erosion of hope, leading to more gambling and drug use and sadly, more begging.

It is a new characteristic of a people and a region, and it is not becoming. (Nor is it funny.)

Chapter Nine

●
●
●
●
●

The Space Between

GROWING UP IN A SMALL college town, I was educated by the tastes and trends of the new south through a
sort of cultural osmosis that occurred in varying doses. I
remember, for instance, making an unannounced visit to
the apartment of two young men, probably seniors, who
attended Ole Miss in the early 1970s and smelling a strange
odor that startled and confused my eight-year-old nose. It
was not until the following year, however, when attending a concert of the pop-hippie band, America—which,
incidentally, my mother had taken me to at age nine,
wrongly thinking it was a sort of patriotic, Broadway style
show—that I put one and another together, recognizing
that my college-aged friends had been smoking marijuana

when their snot-nosed little buddy from across the street knocked on their door.

No wonder they laughed so hard at my fresh, straight-cropped haircut.

"What did you do, get into a fight with a lawnmower?"

They had also asked if I had ever taken a trip, while blindfolded, to a place where the sun don't shine, whatever that meant.

In addition to this, I vividly remember the unique odor that permeated the air when, as a 10-year-old, I spent a memorable, warm, April day on the intramural fields at Ole Miss watching more than 1,000 coeds shake, swizzle and sizzle like angels in a dream. They competed in an annual competition known as Derby Day; I was relishing in this fortuitous parade of beauty while another pungent scent swirled through the air. Only years later, when tasting beer for the first time, did I understand that the kind-of-sweet, kind-of-bitter stench that wafted around the girls like smoke at a barbecue cooking contest, was high-content alcohol vapor, billowing from the breath of these seemingly holy and pure babes, who in actuality were barely wrapped in un-swaddling clothes.

Soon enough, I came to understand that they were these sights, sounds, smells, and, even tastes, which illuminated better than anything else the preferences, as well as the differences, of people, time and place. In accordance, I try to pay careful attention, when given the opportunity, so that I can learn more about the composition of the small world in which we live.

Take New Orleans' Mardi Gras, as an example. The annual celebration with music, parades, parties and excitement in coordination with Fat Tuesday is, by reputation, wild and woolly to the point that some mothers don't want their college age daughters to attend, when invited by classmates. In reality, the heart and history of Mardi Gras beats around upper-economic class families and traditions where children are not only welcomed, but included. For the most part, it is only on and around Bourbon Street, in the French Quarter, where drunken tourists, prostitutes and the like bare their breasts for beads and coconuts. Still others pass out along parade routes, unaware that they are being trampled, fondled, and worse. Simply, not everyone is forgetting their problems; some are creating more.

Likewise, one music festival attended by tens of thousands of young Southerners has little in common with another music festival attended by tens of thousands of young Southerners that is held at precisely the same time during the summer, at a location not more than 70 miles away. I learned this last year during a very unscientific study of Chattanooga's annual Riverbend and Manchester's

-
-
-
-
-
-

annual Bonnaroo, which coincide simultaneously during the first week of June. Both are major festivals built around leading, popular music acts. Both are programmed heavily to appeal to young people living within the region, and both embrace food, frolic and frivolity. But these few similarities aside, the festivals could not be more different. Instead, both are dominated by the personal tastes of the targeted audiences, respectively, and so each boasts drastic differences in flavor of the music and experience.

A four-day event held on a 700-acre farm in Coffee County and featuring over the years such acts as The Allman Brothers Band, Radiohead, The Black Crowes and Widespread Panic, Bonnaroo is for most attendees a fest nourished by marijuana, LSD, and other mind-altering drugs. A kind of Woodstock-reincarnated-at-Green Acres atmosphere, young men and women born in backwoods places like Monticello, Arkansas and Cullman, Alabama parade around with long, unwashed ponytails, tattooed ankles and pierced tongues and nipples, hoping the new friends they meet might mistakenly assume they hail from the likes of Queens, New York or lower Seattle, Washington. If it rains, they run into the elements, arms lifted, hands joined. At night, when the bands quit playing in the wee hours, they retreat on site, to pup tents, sleeping bags, or the dew-soaked ground.

Chattanooga's eight-day Riverbend, on the other hand, features such artists as Kid Rock, Boyz II Men, Big and Rich, Trace Adkins and Pat Benatar. Most patrons sport close-cut, washed hair along with close-cut, stone-washed jean shorts, not to mention trimmed fingernails and snow cone stained tongues. They travel from places like Cleveland, Tennessee and Fort Payne, Alabama and live for this annual eight-day opportunity to indulge on corn dogs, funnel cakes, soft drinks and light, American beer. To be sure, if it looks like rain, they will not get wet. Instead, you will see these couples and families stampeding out the gates toward their cars, Pat Benatar-be-damned. At night, just before the bands play final renditions to meet the city-imposed midnight ending, the veteran attendees gather up their lawn chairs and trash and retreat to the parking lots ahead of the crowd.

The differences between the festivals put me in a bit of a quandary each year of where to go, since I love music and gatherings of southerners. I admit that my tastes lean more toward The Dave Matthews Band and Bela Fleck, as opposed to Cheap Trick and Kid Rock. But, I will also admit to being a little bit sheepish about going to Bonnaroo because of a happenstance meeting in Memphis three years ago with a man 25 years my elder. Making conversation, the old man asked where I lived. When told him that

. . . . .

I lived on a mountain in east Tennessee, he immediately thought of Bonnarroo, the more widely recognized festival in this region. With an Ivy League education and a quit wit, he was an engaging, upwardly-aged professional. But, he was also suspicious, winking and nodding like I knew something that he also did.

"Do you go to the festival?" he asked.

"Which one?" I responded, knowing full well what he meant.

"Bonnaroo, baby," he said, with a twinkle in his eyes. "You know, life is good, livin' is easy...I dig that, you know what I mean?"

Yes, I had a feeling that I knew what he meant. I imagined it went something like this...

Old man takes off from work. Old man loads his wallet with money, his pockets with Viagra, and the trunk of his car with beer. Old man drives to festival. Old man meets younger men, and women. Old man removes money from wallet, buying drugs. Old man gets stoned, again and again. Old man shares drugs with younger men, and women. Old man inserts himself into hemp heavy younger woman. Old man makes more new friends, and more new friends. Old man's heart almost stops beating. Younger woman gives him mouth to mouth. Old man sees a vision. Old man comes to. Younger woman gives him mouth to penis. Old man gets stoned again. Old man gets in his car. Old man drives home, smiling, remembering all the great hallucinations had by all.

You may laugh, but I'm not exactly sure why, considering that for four days each year, when the farm in Coffee County transforms into a little Amsterdam for four days, the old man, and any of the other thousands of attendees, can purchase and ingest any illegal substance desired with little threat of conflict with the law. Local authorities, of course, are present, and try to show church-going citizens who live nearby that they really do want to put a dent in the narcotics traffic that comes to the area for the festival, confiscating 328 hits of LSD here, or 10 grams of cocaine there.

After one particularly gratifying bust, the sheriff called a news conference, announcing that one van with a Florida tag was pulled over on Highway 49 because of suspicious driving. Oddly enough, the attending officer smelled something. Upon asking the driver to step out of the vehicle, eight baggies of marijuana fell to the ground. The officer called in reinforcement. An arrest was made. For the press announcement, the entire force was summoned. They smiled for the cameras, then went to Milly's diner for pie a la mode to toast the big day. Meanwhile, two tons of cocaine, four bales of marijuana and 14,000

•
•
•
•
•
•

hits of LSD entered Coffee County via semi-trick. The driver apparently pulled right up to the festival gate and opened the hatch, while dealers evenly divided the goods among themselves.

Realistically, of course, there is little that can be done when so many sellers with so many drugs convene at one, small rural location. Consider only that at the end of the 2005 festival, one journalist wrote that, despite her humble and fairly conservative upbringing, she had grown accustomed after four days of Bonnaroo to routinely being offered drugs for sale and was no longer surprised to see a man smoking a strange red pipe, obviously not intended for tobacco use. Another scribe noted that after a Bonnaroo concert by The Dave Matthews Band, some nudity was seen, but mostly, "there were lots and lots of people staggering about." One can only imagine that the patrons were looking at each other, never saying a thing, wondering what the other was thinking, as the crimes between them grew deeper. Even a story in the *Manchester Times*, Coffee County's largest newspaper, stated that "the odor of marijuana was overpowering on the grounds as festival attendees openly ignored the Bonnaroo prohibition on illegal substances."

Then the news was reported that Florida State University's starting quarterback from 2004 was arrested by

Tallahassee police for strange behavior which included him proclaiming that he was God, while crouching on all fours in the street with no shirt and no shoes on. His roommates reportedly told authorities the quarterback had just returned from Bonnaroo.

Jimi Hendrix or Jim Morrison, I could understand, but God?

Thank goodness for Riverbend.

Okay, so it features worn out rockers and culture-confused rappers, but when I approached a beer stand at Chattanooga's festival the first time I attended, at the same time shunning Bonnaroo going on across the Cumberland Plateau, I was carded for age identification, despite being almost 40-years-old with thinning hair and obvious, saggy-male bosoms. And, to my further surprise, beer lines were almost non-existent, despite a record crowd soaring over 100,000. It was much more difficult, however, to purchase the festival foods of choice, including, belch, corndogs and funnel cakes.

Admittedly, Riverbend fare is not exactly heart-wise, but no matter how many funnel cakes and beer a person consumes, hallucination should not be a side effect; bloating, perhaps.

In my visits to Chattanooga's riverfront festival, I don't recall seeing any out-of-control drunks, nor have I witnessed

· · · · ·

anything more disturbing than a few boys, probably age 15, coolly smoking cigarettes. So Kid Rock screamed some four-letter expletives from the stage...at Bonnaroo, if one peered long enough through the purple haze, they could witness some of this foulness in action.

Excuse me, is that a bong in your pocket, or are you just glad to see me?

Riverbend's tired lineup of musical acts might be somewhat of a heartbreaker to me and others who consider themselves aficionados, but I, for one, will admit to having myself a big and rich time each time out. Besides, watching and listening to acts like an extremely large black man named Cowboy Troy rapping on stage to traditional country chords is mind-expanding enough for me.

Chapter Ten

.
.
.
.
.

Our New Sweet Tea: Merlot

AS WITH ALL DISTINCTIVE CULTURAL regions and people in the world, the South is known for its own indigenous food and drink, which crystallize its flavor and spirit with unhealthy doses of processed sugar and saturated fat. From low country grits to Mississippi Delta fried catfish to Memphis barbecue, the fare has been enjoyed by multitudes for generations, leaping across social and economic divides with the same unbridled ease as music made by Elvis or B.B. King.

As an example, throughout the second half of the 20th century, it would be completely common for a nice restaurant in a predominantly white area of Spartanburg, South Carolina to serve fried pork chops as a featured entrée

-
-
-
-
-

on the menu, just as the same meal could be ordered at a down-home restaurant in a predominantly black area of North Charleston. One of the pork chop dishes might be accompanied with a side of field greens doused in Louisiana hot sauce, while the other was served with, say, a side of butter-infused mashed potatoes. However, both would likely be washed down with the same beverage—sweetened ice tea.

As arguably the most renowned and ubiquitous of all our region's ingestibles, sweet tea is to the South what coffee is to Seattle and what cheese is to Holland—a signature serving that is expected, be it at the formal dinner table or an impromptu porch sitting. Although it has not been a tradition as long as some may surmise, black tea sweetened with spoonfuls of sugar, poured over ice and topped off in the glass with a wedge of lemon became an integral part of life for many in Dixie, through socialization and meals, in the 1930s and 1940s.

The origin of this trend dates back two centuries, to the late 1700s, when a French explorer and botanist brought the first tea plant to the United States, planting it near Charleston, South Carolina. The state became the first and only in America to produce tea commercially, and although it never competed in volume with imports from places like India, the domestic production certainly fostered creativity in uses throughout the region. This was particularly true in the late 1800s, when, due to improvements in refrigeration and freezing, iced tea gained in popularity, particularly in the form of liquor-laced, sweetened tea punches.

Black tea over ice emerged over green tea as the clear Southern favorite—particularly when green tea imports were not readily available during World War II—and many South Carolinians, particularly the more affluent, for whom the price of sugar was not an issue, began leaving the liquor out of the recipe, concocting instead a sugary drink suitable for the entire family. Sweet black tea over ice was served at the dinner table, just as it was served in the early evening during the beverage hour.

As sugar became more affordable for the masses in the latter half of the 20th century, a fondness of sweat tea spread from South Carolina to Atlanta to New Orleans to Memphis and beyond. It was consumed on the farm, in the city, and in Delta mansions. When the days turned hot, leaving people with little to do but sit outside on the porch and tell stories, the beverage they sipped was quite often sweat tea; something so simple, yet complex enough that recipes were published extensively in church and ladies' society cookbooks.

"TEA—Freshly brewed tea, after three to five minutes' infusion, is essential if a good quality is desired. The water,

.
.
.
.
.

as for coffee, should be freshly boiled and poured over the tea for this short time . . . The tea leaves may be removed when the desired strength is obtained . . . Tea, when it is to be iced, should be made much stronger, to allow for the ice used in chilling . . . To sweeten tea for an iced drink - less sugar is required if put in while tea is hot, but often too much is made and sweetened, so in the end there is more often a waste than saving . . . Iced tea should be served with or without lemon, with a sprig of mint, a strawberry, a cherry, a slice of orange, or pineapple. This may be fresh or canned fruit. Milk is not used in iced tea."

Thank goodness all that was clarified so meticulously, or else, the inexperienced might have ruined a good, new trend by doing something foolish like pouring a cup of milk into their tea or dropping pecans into the sweetened concoction instead of fruit.

As it was, the instructions were such that anybody who could operate a stove-top burner and wield a measuring cup could enjoy sweat tea, and, thus, a tradition was born. My mother made it, as did her mother, and I recall watching them brew and mix their personal recipe as daily routine: Water boiled, two bags of tea brewed, more water added to fill the pitcher, and a half-pound of sugar stirred into it. That's right, half a pound. At times, the concoction was so sweat that it rolled in my mouth as something tasting more akin to taffy than tea, but I always finished the glass and always came back for more, especially when my father laced it with freshly-picked mint from the garden.

I do remember being surprised, though, when I was 12-years-old and had a friend staying over for the night who had moved to town a few months before from out west. A military child, his parents were both birthed and reared in the North, leaving the habits of the South foreign to him. At the dinner table, my mother served him a glass of ice tea. He took one drink, and proceeded to spew it back out onto to his plate, into his lap, and across the table.

"Shit!" he uttered.

He was the first friend to cuss in our Baptist home in front of my parents, but it was okay, even understandable, considering that he professed to never having tasted sweet tea before. He didn't seem interested to ever taste it again, noting that the drink was so laden with sugar that his palate had actually registered the drink as something drowned in a salty, bitter flavor.

My friend moved from the South in the 1980s, and as far as I know, he has not been back. But if he does return, I'm sure he will be pleased to find that, although sweet tea still holds the reputation being the South's drink of choice in the 21st century, this in effect is not true whatsoever. Sure, in many locally-owned diners and cafes and in homes from McComb, Mississippi to Ocala, Florida, tea is doused heavily with sugar before being served over ice, but for the most part, the developing culture of the new, new South has a decidedly different flavor.

How this happened dates back to the last decade, just before the turn of the century, when Outback Steakhouses began popping up across the region quicker than you can say "bloomin' onion". Many of the locations serve sweetened tea, while others did not, but it didn't matter for long. When other large-scale restaurant-chain competitors, like Macaroni Grill, began opening in cities like Montgomery, Alabama and Knoxville, Tennessee, bringing what was previously considered to be higher-end fare to the grub-experts of the Southern middle class, different menu choices inevitably followed.

Take wine, for instance. The last region of America, not surprisingly, to catch onto the burgeoning trend of wine was the South. It was just 20 years ago, for instance, that I recall going to parties at the homes of people who should have known better than to serve wine from cardboard boxes, as opposed to decanters. There was none of this, "Would you like a glass of Sbragia 2002 Rancho del Oso Cabernet Sauvignon or a glass of Calera 2001 Mt. Harlan Jensen Vineyard Pinot Noir?" silliness. It was more, "Yes, those are nice goldfish in the built-in pond in my living room, but ease back to the kitchen with me so I can glug, glug, glug you out a glassful of Chablis from that oversize box that I squeezed into the fridge last night, barely leaving room for the cheese plate."

It is true, of course, that the masses have not exactly turned into connoisseurs; quite the opposite, in fact. But, when chain restaurants began peddling merlot as a featured menu item, people wobbly stood up and took notice, finding pleasure that its medium body looked and smelled like contemporary culture. Therefore, it was not long before oversize, empty bottles, pegged as "dead soldiers" and featuring labels like Meridian and Woodbridge, became commonplace around the Southern dinner table, just as they become commonplace on front porches and around the bar in the men's golf club grill and in the kitchen of condos occupied by hordes of vacationing women.

Now, attendees of parties in the South don't have to fear being served wine from a cardboard box. Even members of the clanky young adult Sunday School Class from First Baptist Church of Wherever will even see fit to serve corked bottles of wine and none of that screw top stuff or vino-in-a-box, at the annual Christmas party. Of course, the non-drinking attendees will have to navigate a maze of emotionally-charged conversations with peers, who flash red-stained teeth and reek of sour-grape breath.

•
•
•
•
•

Yes, Virginia, that story was funny, until, that is, you smiled broadly in exclamation. Your mouth could use a little repentance, and a shot of fluoride.

And wine isn't the only taste Southerners have acquired from the contemporary infusion of chain restaurants, revealing the cuisine of such mesmerizing places as Australia, Italy, China and Texas de Brazil. Why, I was reading in my daily newspaper just the other day a comment from the executive chef of a prominent, metropolitan country club in the South. When asked about his favorite restaurant, other than the club, he plainly stated that Outback "has the best crab legs" and that he took his daughter there at every opportunity for seafood. Never mind that there are at least two restaurants in town that could hold their own in Manhattan; the best food this chef could name was from a chain restaurant with the motto "No rules, just right."

That's exactly why, in the South, so many cloistered diets, typically built around such hometown staples as macaroni and cheese, chicken strips, pork chops, rice, barbecue, potato chips and the like, are now expanding, courtesy of this new brand of exotic, franchised options. I learned this first hand one evening, while dining at a nice restaurant located along on the Alabama Gulf Coast.

It was summertime, in the season just before a great hurricane descended upon the region, ruining all things good and tacky with unimaginable winds and waves. And it was evening, following a day in which a searing sun shone, crystal waters sparkled as the browning waters of the nearby Mobile Bay stayed, well, at bay, and country girls flaunted somewhat-perky bosoms, and bottoms split in string bikinis bounced around on the outside patio at the FloraBama lounge while music played and sunburned men smoked Marlboro's and marveled.

Seated at a table with my wife and children, I could not help but overhear and watch two families seated at an adjacent table. They looked like a million bucks; faces freshly flushed with sun and dressed each in varying garments of white linen. They numbered 10 in all, four adults and six children, and they had obviously just come from a sunset photo shoot on the beach. Collectively and as individuals, they were beautiful, shining testaments to the benefits of new-South economics, because, as I listened to them talk, it was apparent that, despite appearances, they remained a bit like torn cardboard, generally smooth, but rough around the edges.

"Dillon," one of the women blared to a child. "Whatcha gonna eat? You'll like 'em popcorn shrimp, dontcha think?"

Once it was decided what food the children would order, the adults launched into a painful dialogue about

•
•
•
•
•

ordering that ran from suspicion, perception and fact in a very slippery manner. One man wanted steak, but a woman—apparently his wife—thought he ate steak too often.

"Git sommen different for a change," she said. "I like steak, too, but I'm not gonna order it just 'cause it's on the menu."

"What're you goin' to order?"

"Well, I'm thinking about getting the *sal*mon," she said.

"*Sal*mon? You don't eat *sal*mon."

"Yeah, don't you remember?" she said. "I got it once at Outback Steakhouse. It was good, too."

When the waitress came to take their orders, the man did indeed choose steak. But, to the woman's credit, she branched out, ordering *sal*mon fillet. Of course, she also asked for a glass of merlot, which, to the pleasure of my listening ears, she properly pronounced.

Chapter Eleven

•
•
•
•
•
•

Honky Tonk Angel

THE BACKWOODS BARROOM HAS LONG been an attraction for the professional southern male when traveling among friends or straying unescorted from his more urban, natural surroundings. Like a circus to a child, the honky tonk and its clientele are a fascination and entertainment of odd dimensions to the southern male, as well as a distraction, albeit brief, from the structured rigors and hearty pressures of everyday life and responsibility.

Back in the day, such establishments were frequented mostly by locals, with the more educated, higher earning urbanized males spending their time in private clubs and public places of better repute. But as the city has expanded closer to the country in recent years, the number of chain establishments serving alcohol by the gallons has escalated on the fringes of once-isolated communities, and, consequently, the number of backwoods barrooms has dwindled, making them coveted, if not craved. This fact, combined with ever-increasing pressures on the professional to dress one way, act one way and earn one way, has only intensified the southern male's drive to search out and partake in a hob-knobbing, low-brow barroom, when the rare opportunity presents itself.

It's not trouble or physical altercations that these men seek, since that can be found on any corner of any city or town from Pensacola, Florida to Fayetteville, Arkansas—that is, if one had such a desire. Instead, the southern male heads once or twice a year to backwoods honky tonks for the sake of momentary escapism, a kind of Disney for Dads, where for a dizzying spell cold beer tastes colder, twangy music actually sounds good, and the barmaids in tank-tops seem to have full sets of teeth—but heed my advice, friend: look but don't touch. This honky tonk experience is partly an ego boost, reminding urban men of who they are not, and partly a dose of reality reminding them of whom they could've been, and it can all be packaged in three D's that characterize any true, honky tonk demagogue—dancing, dialogue and drunk.

One friend, Jeff, who works as a high-powered financier

in Nashville by day and goes home to a beautiful wife and two attractive, toddler-aged children at night, lives the textbook life of having a seven-figure income, complete with a Belle Meade house and two vacation homes. Because he gets bored walking the same walk and talking the same talk, trips to backwoods barrooms when traveling with friends on hunting or golf trips have become mandatory. Each time, it seems, he goes through the same drill. Immediately after entering, he seeks a lonely local cowpoke and offers to buy him drinks, an act that repeats itself. Like a squirrel digging for buried nuts, Jeff keeps asking the cowpoke questions like what he does for fun and which girls in the building like to dance—you know, the fatty morsels of information.

On a recent and somewhat memorable trip that I happened to be along for, I was taken to a place called Mike's on the River, somewhere in south Georgia. It didn't take Jeff long to scout out the right cowpoke for prodding. The man was seated alone, facing the country band at a long, cafeteria-style table. Wearing the standard-issue outfit with cowboy hat, a white shirt buttoned low enough to reveal his thick, gold chain and a barrel chest grown with gnarly hairs, and blue jeans held up with a big-buckled belt that was nearly engulfed by his overhanging belly, this fella, Bobby, was easy prey. He had a round face and a thick mustache and a big, easy smile.

-
-
-
-
-

Jeff offered to buy him a drink, but Bobby said no thank you, he was fine with his beer. Jeff offered again, but Bobby said no thank you, he did not need to do that. Jeff offered again, and Bobby said, okay, I'll just have a margarita on the rocks with salt around the glass. When the waitress came, Jeff offered to buy Bobby some food, a gesture which was readily accepted.

"Bring me some of them shrimp cocktail," he said, "and I'll also have a grilled cheese, with cheese sticks and a cup of that marinara sauce on the side."

Why Bobby thought the shrimp cocktail from Mike's on the River—a place where nobody else dared to eat despite it being just 8:45 p.m.—would be good idea, I don't know, but he mowed them down, just as he did the rest of the food and the drink. Four margaritas later (all on Jeff's tab), he declared it was time to "start hittin' some shooters," ordering a round for everybody in sight—naturally, on Jeff's tab. Once he had downed a couple of these, he stood up, wobbly, and kept talking to anyone who would listen while dancing in place. Jeff reached for Bobby's cowboy hat, which he rather easily allowed to be lifted from his head, a fact that utterly disappointed Jeff.

"Any roughneck that gives up his hat ain't really a roughneck at all," he said.

It was true that, when Bobby repeatedly put his arms

around our necks to move closer while telling a story, his hands did seem unreasonably soft. And the dance floor was full of boot-scooting women, yet for Bobby, it seemed perfectly natural to focus on us. Jeff, on the other hand, was getting his typical itch, pledging to the group that "he was going to find the ugliest bitch in the house" and ask her to dance. He tried once, tried again and three times a lady but was shot down each time, presumably because they had non-dancing boyfriends back at a table.

Wobbly Bobby seemed to thoroughly enjoy the rejections, and, as the evening came to a close, he moved in closer to Jeff, putting his arm around him and suggesting they "crash the stage" for the final number. Jeff loved the idea, and they moved front and center of the band, stepping onto the stage arm in arm, uninvited as the band erupted into the closing tune, a cover of the Commodore's "Brick House." Band members bristled at first at the intrusion, but kept on playing nonetheless. Jeff claimed a position at the front of the stage, while Bobby nestled in just behind him. They were dancing and singing and movin' to the groovin' when just then, it hit me. Jeff turned around and grabbed Bobby's hat, removing it and placing it on his head. Bobby laughed, and as Jeff turned back around, hat on head, for more singing, Bobby moved in closer and started thrusting his lower half forward while cracking an imaginary whip to the beat.

.
.
.
.
.

This cowpoke was not right.

But they kept singing and dancing and having a big old time, Jeff completely unaware that Bobby was making an end run. By the climatic finish of the song, Bobby was having himself a friction dance on Jeff's backside and as the final chords were strummed, he wrapped his arms around Jeff's waist, clinging tightly. At this moment, the male dancers fell completely backwards, off the stage, with Jeff landing in Bobby's arms, his body clasped between Bobby's legs like a board in a vice grip. Hoping to avoid a barroom brawl, I quickly whisked Jeff from the floor, bid Bobby adieu, and fled the scene, with friend in tow.

"Bobby…he was nice," Jeff said in a slur, from the backseat of the car, "a pretty good cowboy after all."

However, the tale of Bobby's brief, innocent crush on Jeff seems like a children's bedtime story when compared to this one experience several men from Memphis brought home from a backwoods barroom during a hunting trip in eastern Arkansas. Six of them, including my friend Mitch, had fled for three days in pursuit of ducks and geese, bunking together at a Best Western located off Interstate 40. On the final afternoon, following a morning hunt, there was little to do but drink, so they loaded up on beer and whiskey and sat in folding chairs around their cars in the motel parking lot, drinking and telling stories and passing time. By nightfall, they were feeling limber and antsy for conversation other than their own, so they inquired at the front desk about local bars. There was only one, they were told, and it was out in the county, some 17 miles away. No problem, the hunters replied, just give us directions.

Since they arrived at the honky tonk early and considering it was a week night, there were only four other stragglers there. The waitress who served them turned out to be a looker by the accounts of all six, though you must take into consideration their impaired judgment. Telling the inquiring men she was in her 40s, Jennie had shoulder length bleach-blonde hair and a taut figure highlighted by a short and tight blue jean skirt and a tight t-shirt. Because the guys had nothing better to do in the bar, they passed time by continuing bold, brash-talking games started in the parking lot. It was one bet after another, each one trying to show up the rest.

"I'll bet you five bucks that fella behind the bar lights up a cigarette within three minutes."

"I'll bet you a dollar John will throw up before the night is over."

"I'll bet you 50 my wife ices me for two full days when I get home."

Eavesdropping as she served round after round of drinks,

.
.
.
.
.

Jennie apparently heard the opening she was looking for, interrupting the conversation with a bet of her own.

"You boys like to bet?" she said.

"Sure," said Mitch. "Whatcha got?"

"Well," she said, "I'll bet you boys one hundred bucks that I can stand on one side of a car in the parking lot and pee-pee completely over it,"

"C'mon," said another.

"Like I said," Jennie repeated slowly. "I'll bet you a hundred bucks that I can pee-pee over a car in the parking lot."

Mitch has never been known to be the smartest of men, but he knew enough to strongly suspect that any woman who said she could urinate over a car was absolutely out of her mind. The trick would be hard enough for a man, who benefits from having an urethra strung through a six-inch hose, which is a convenient device for aiming left, right and even high. A woman, on the other hand, is at a considerable disadvantage, considering her urethra has severely limited, if any, maneuverability. Even a bunch of drunken men know that. So, one by one, they reached into their pockets, slapping down bills on the table ranging from $20 to $50. In all, they collected $220, despite the fact that the waitress had only suggested betting $100. But, whatever, it was a bar, and the bet was absurd, so nobody minded.

"Let me get this straight," Jennie said, "just so there are no hurt feelings. If I got out this door, pull my drawers down, and pee-pee completely over one of them cars out there, you boys are gonna give me this here money, no hassle, no hard feelings?"

"Let's do it," Mitch said, pounding his fist on the table.

The men scrambled from their chairs, whooping and hollering, and followed Jennie out the door. Of course, they were followed by the bartender and the other handful of patrons who were passing time in the honky tonk. With everyone watching, Jennie was said to have wasted no time, pulling down her thigh-length skirt and panties, but leaving her black waitress apron tied firmly tied around her mid-section. Standing together at the front of the car, under the dim light of a street lamp, they cracked one joke after another, about pee this and pee that, ultimately urging Jennie to spray away with her best shot.

By this time she had heard enough, so she sat on the ground, leaned back, flipped her apron up around her chest, threw her legs behind her head, clinched her labia with both hands as if to create an effect like a nozzle on the end of a hose, and pushed from her bladder with all her might.

The first trickle of spray slapped the small car's passenger door with enough force to make a thump, thump sound.

Within seconds, however, she had adjusted the flow with applied pressure, providing enough resistance and guidance that a stream of urine did indeed shoot up and over the car, splashing on the other side in the gravel drive, like water spouting from a fountain. Mitch and the boys were mesmerized and speechless.

Inside, after handing Jennie two 50 dollar bills and four 20s, they found, as they talked among themselves, that they had been strangely affected by the odd talent that had just swept away their cash. Spurred by sexual stimulation and a bit of disgust, their talk began to turn from casual bets to sex, and a few suggested that picking up a couple of girls before going home might be nice. They didn't mean it, of course. This was purely the result of eight hours of alcohol consumption and the sight of a naked waitress urinating over a car.

However, they had a hard time convincing Jennie of that. Eavesdropping once again, she sashayed on over and let them know right then and there that pee-peeing over a car was not the only trick she could perform with her private parts. But having seen what they just saw, the guys knew better than to ask about, or issue to the waitress a sexual challenge of any sort.

"We'll just take the check," Mitch said.

Chapter Twelve

•
•
•
•
•
•

Let it Snow,
'Cause the Boys Got Cabin Fever

ONE QUALITY OF SOUTHERNERS THAT has not changed much over time is an obsession with all things weather-related. Perhaps this climatalogical infatuation dates back generations to the days when most living below the Mason-Dixon Line were either directly involved in agriculture or closely related to someone who was. Whether or not it rained at precisely the right time or whether the temperature was too high, or too low at precisely the wrong time, largely dictated the economics of the south.

If families were not into farming, they were likely involved with community businesses such as banks and grocery stores that that either soared or suffered as a result of how the seasonal winds had blown. The weather mattered, a lot, and this was instilled to the point that still today, when the vast majority of families in these times have little more than a potted tomato plant on the patio in terms of vegetational concern, people still talk about and worry, arguably excessively, about the weather. It might rain, they say. There's going to be a frost, they say.

I'm no different than most of my southern peers in that I watch the weather daily, frequently cross-checking one forecast against another in formulaic style so that a derivative conclusion can be reached and I talk hours on end with anyone who will listen about whether or not the atmospheric state at hand could be improved, or not, with variations in temperature or moisture. More times than not, considering that the south is warmer region of the United States and is also buffered by the waters from the Gulf of Mexico, it is not the heat, but the humidity.

If only, we often say.

But on a winter day last year, with the temperature hovering close to 50 degrees, it definitely wasn't the heat that confounded me so but the stupidity. Because, following a long mountain walk on the most beautiful winter day one could ask for, no matter how hard I tried that day to figure out why my body felt like it had been run through a dehydrating machine, I could not.

My mouth was so dry that my tongue felt like it had been mysteriously exchanged for a two-sided piece of sandpaper. My normally over-moist epidermis crawled with a static itch, while what remains of the hair of my head clung so tightly to the cranium it was as if it had been smothered with plastic wrap. I felt more like I was suited for joining dried fruit in a small baggy than flourishing in the open air as a living, breathing, hydrogenated being. Still, I could not figure out why I had become akin to a walking, talking piece of kindling, in need of a burn-warning sign attachment.

CAUTION: *You are approaching a highly flammable human. No smoking allowed.*

But when I settled down for lunch with a tall glass of iced black tea in front of a television tuned to a mid-day news program, the reason for my dryness revealed itself like an oversize yacht moored downtown along the banks of the Mississippi River. With the temperature in the Tennessee Valley hovering in the low 50s, the dew point—the temperature at which condensation of water held in the air occurs—registered at a strikingly low 19 degrees, translating into a very un-southern-like relative humidity reading of 22 percent. Rarely in the south, be it winter, summer or fall, does the temperature and dew point combine in the middle of the day to result in such

• • • •

a low humidity reading; in the Rocky Mountains, yes; in the Cumberland Plateau, no.

That's sophisticated weather jargon, I know, talking about dew point. I have been advised by weather professionals, as well as my wife, that most people care to discuss only the result, and the impacts, not the technicalities. So, suffice it to say that, on the extraordinary day when I was walking along a mountain located deep in the heart of Dixie, the air was so dry that one could have turned a plum into a prune on a sidewalk, if one wanted to.

I am not a fruit, however, and therefore the extreme and unusual dryness caught me quite off guard since drying out was not a priority. After living exclusively in the south for more than 40 years, I have become somewhat like a whale in the ocean: this oxygen-breathing mammal needs a little water in the air.

There can be too much of a good thing, of course. In the summer, for instance, when the air contains so much moisture that my sunglasses fog up during a slight and easy stroll, I long for moderation, a time when sweat that builds on the brow does not meet so much resistance that it cannot evaporate in reasonable time. I do like to sweat, a little, but not so much so that it rolls down my back and channels into my crack. It does admittedly get a bit old in the dead of summer when I'm at a party, trying to imbibe and have good conversation, when my face appears to be formed of a thousand tiny droplets and the sweat collecting underneath my arms do so in such quantity that rings big enough to serve the Barnum and Bailey Circus form down to my belt-line.

But, even despite these extremes when a long July runs into an even longer August, the humidity is still acceptable because it is what I have come to know and expect through years of acclimation. One, for instance, would not think that a woman would be more comfortable in a brassiere or a man in a necktie, yet despite periods of rebellion, they never go away because, despite complaints, people have adapted to them to the point of a kind of ensnared comfort.

Similarly, the unusual and unexpected spell of air that was so dry it more belonged atop a Canadian mountain than in the Tennessee River region of the southeast was a reminder to me of the old saying, "be careful what you wish for." My occasional thoughts and dreams of having drier air grace me at home were met with harsh reality on my morning walk that day last winter. By all accounts, it was glorious, with a shining sun warming the vernal equinox, but, inexplicably, I kept having the desire to lie down on the sidewalk and ask strange passers-by to find a mop, get it wet, and swab me down.

-
-
-
-
-

A lack of humidity or a little rain in the forecast is nothing, however, to the frenzy that engulfs the region when snow is in the forecast. Normally as placid as a hound dog lying in a hot summer sun, today's southerner makes a startling change in upon there mere mention of the chance for snow in their area. Rednecks, of course, have gotten worked up about snow for as long as anyone can remember, yet that was nothing in comparison to the jitters obtained over the potential fluffy, frozen precipitation in these times. The reason for this perceptible increase in excitability is due, no doubt, to effects from global warming and El Nina, both firmly in place since the turn of the century.

With the jet stream riding high near Canada for the majority of winter days and a warm, offshore air flow moving west to east from the waters of the South Pacific, winter in Dixie, from Memphis to Atlanta, has been as tame and unimpressive as a University of Alabama coed at 7:00 a.m. following a night game—making snowflakes in abundance more rare than at any other time in record. Not since the spring blizzard of 1993 dropped 20 inches of snow on Chattanooga, 15 inches on Birmingham and more than a foot on parts in between these anchors of fiefdom, has the South gotten walloped by a widespread, heavy falling of the white stuff. Sure, there have been four inches here or an isolated nine inches there, but nothing farfetched, covering state line after state line, like the snows many citizens of the northern South became accustomed to every two or three years since the sixties.

Any outsider of the South reading this book may assume that our lack of frozen precipitation may be more of a blessing than curse, but anybody who's spent much time in the bowels of America understands that too many years without significant snowfall makes the natives restless. Sure, they wish they could act like they don't want snow or don't care if it falls from the sky and sticks, even briefly, to the ground. But as soon as a weatherman in some place like Little Rock, Arkansas or Columbia, South Carolina makes mention of a legitimate chance for accumulating snow—a half-inch, four inches; it doesn't matter—people start hopping and buzzing around, resembling more of the LSU kickoff squad in Death Valley at 7:30 on a Saturday night than calcified citizens of the South. Frenzied fools are making trips to the grocery for excessive milk, bread and snacks, planning for contingency if school or work is cancelled and pacing back and forth to televisions for updated weather forecasts.

"It looks like we really *might* get a little bit this time," one hopeful reports to another, while coolly trying to act like they really don't care if it happens.

Only an outsider would fall for such a seemingly

ambivalent attitude. Any Southerner worth their grits loves a good snowfall, period, amen, pass the cornbread. That's all there is to it. That's why there's a significant rise in blood pressure and general level of activity in communities like Shreveport, Louisiana, and Columbus, Mississippi, when the official forecast moves to within 48 hours of a distinct possibility.

It's gonna snow, it's gonna snow. Hang fire, it's gonna snow.

It rarely does, though, considering that conditions have to be just absolutely right for the meteorological phenomenon to occur. The ingredients: rising moisture from the south, converging with cold air moving in from the north that's deep enough in layer so that sleet pellets, freezing rain, or merely cold drizzle are avoided. Typically, the local weather station's meteorologist, Tom—who is really just a B-minus journalism graduate of The University of Southern Mississippi with a bad hair-do, rather than an educated authority climatologically inclined—calls for serious snow two or three times per year in all parts north of a line running from Texarkana to Montgomery, by dramatically reading a three-paragraph computer printout generated by the National Weather Service.

"Big changes may be on the way," the news anchor announces, so let's go to Chief Meteorologist Tom in the weather center for the official word on what may transpire in the next three days."

"Thanks, John!" Meteorologist Tom belts out, all too eagerly. "I was over at Central Elementary today speaking to some children about what makes the weather, and I got to watch children on the playground enjoying this 60 degree day. But that's all about to change, because…hmm mmm…"

It is at this point that viewers might be best served if Meteorologist Tom would just come clean, telling the viewing public that he doesn't know any more about the weather forecast than they can find through two clicks on the Internet; that he is just four years removed from college, a period in which he spent most of his time hanging his penis through a hole in the stall door at a public library in Hattiesburg, soliciting unseen strangers to use it as practice for apple-bobbing contests that might arise in the future. Or maybe not. That's just what I expect from this kind of guy.

If he came clean with viewers, Meteorologist Tom might say something more along the lines of: "Thanks, John. I was over at Central Elementary today, trying to act like I knew something about the weather, but all I could think about were those cute little boys I saw running around on the playground. As for a change in the weather, I haven't

•
•
•
•
•

a fucking clue. So I'm just going to drool over this little statement that I have here in my hand from the weather service..."

But every now and then, in spite of flimsy meteorological interpretations by weathermen like Tom, the moons align over a place like Memphis, which is why the Tennessee city averages 5.5 inches of snowfall per year (although it should be noted that the average since the turn of the century is far less). When that happens, it is each person for his or her own, with all food absent from supermarket shelves and everything, everywhere canceled, from ballet classes to high school classes to mandatory DUI classes. No senior night bingo, no Girl Scout bake sale and no third shift at the factory. Children will find a hill and try to sled on everything from state-of-the-art sleds to box tops to trash can lids. Women will make bake something hot that fills the kitchen with a pleasant aroma, and men will crank up their trucks and ride. Looking for what, I don't know, but they will be riding, and looking, riding and looking.

In their trucks, these men will take on a different persona. It is as if the purity of the white stuff surrounding them permeates a certain kindness and calmness into their hardened, roughneck souls. Normally the types of men one might try to avoid, they become snow saints of the season, offering help in the form of tows, pushes or road flares. The slow, methodical pace in which these men travel the roads compares nothing with the fast, roaring mode of getting from one point to another that they typically adhere to. Likewise, their personalities morph, for reasons inexplicable to even the most studious scholars of Southern behavior.

There's none of that honking, move-over-bitch-before-I-run-your-high-fallutin-ass-over attitude. Instead, it's more: "I spec you could make it back awwight if you go yonder way. We just came through there, and, really, them roads ain't that bad. Be careful now. Have a good day." (*Gentle nod, combined with a slight tip of a John Deere cap*).

Nothing is ever perfect, however, and there is typically some Northerner nearby to throw salt on the South's frozen party. It is as predictable to us as the decision made each February by a big, blue chip high school football lineman torn between signing a scholarship with Vanderbilt or Alabama. Always, he will end up going with the Crimson Tide, just as some Northerner will predictably always condemn our snow.

"Where I come from," they will say, "people would laugh at this. This…this is nothing."

One would think from such statements that everybody who grew up in the North, but now live in the South, used to routinely get a foot of snow and drive successfully

.
.
.
.
.

through it to un-cancelled work, blindfolded, while bal-
ancing crates of un-cracked eggs on the roof of their car.

And they wonder why it's so hard to make friends down
here.

"Yes, honey, I *did* like Bob. But, after it snowed last year,
I never looked at him the same."

Perhaps that is why the Chattanooga area, where I currently live, is such a homogeneous Southern place. In the
bowels of the Tennessee Valley, it rarely snows more than
a flake or few. One might think otherwise since snow so
routinely and beautifully falls in the nearby higher eleva-
tions, but in the valley region, less snow falls annually than
is received in northern Mississippi and northern Alabama.
It has long been this way, the reason having everything
to do with the Cumberland Plateau to the west and the
Appalachian Mountains to the east. In winter, when cold
air needed for snowmaking moves in from the west, the
plateau serves as barrier, blocking just enough chill to make
the difference. Or, later in winter, during the less-frequent
times that a high pressure sits to the north of the region,
funneling cold air south, the Appalachian Mountains have
exactly the same effect on the city, only in reverse. Add to
these factors global warming and El Nina, and one can see
why no measurable snow has been recorded in the valley
since 2002.

However, every now and then, there's enough cold air to overcome the negating factors, which surges over the hills and into the valley allowing a brief, uniquely Southern metamorphosis to take place. I look out the window, seeing flakes start to fall, and I know that men in the area already have an itchy finger wrapped around the ignition key of their truck. Becoming subdued, they just wait for the figurative horn to sound and the announcement to be made, summoning them, just as others are summoned everywhere in Dixie when falling snow reaches the ground in collecting quantity.

Gentlemen, start your engines.

Chapter Thirteen

. . . . .

Dr. Bubba Drives a Truck

AS THE SOUTHERN MALE BECAME urbanized in the latter portion of the 20th century—thanks to the gentrification of metropolitan areas like Atlanta and Birmingham, easy-to-use and inexpensive means of communication like the internet and mobile telephones, and the flow of jobs from farms to the city—an internal struggle ensued to cling to elements of rural manhood, more specifically ruggedness, toughness and a connection to the land.

For instance, it became fine for Bubba, who grew up on the outskirts of Dothan, Alabama but who now lives in the heart of Mobile, to enjoy polenta as a side dish at dinner and to read GQ magazine during breaks at the hospital from his job as the leading regional heart surgeon.

•
•
•
•
•

You might guess, too, that Bubba had liposuction in 1999 to vacuum a couple of inches off his waist, so he wouldn't end up like his daddy, unable to see his toes while standing upright and unable to cover his butt crack while seated.

Though he never admitted it out loud, Bubba also proved through his actions that he firmly believed there was a limit to how soft and feminine a man should be, regardless of changing times and a kinder, gentler South. That's why, with all available free time between office appointments, surgeries, workouts at the gym and detoxifying, exfoliating, and ginger and sassafras rub downs at the day spa, he went in search of ways to embellish manhood through southern muskique, grabbing and tightly hold onto to any secretions, hobbies or other manly enhancements that seemed to do the aura-stimulating trick.

He had never liked hunting, for example, preferring as a young man to sleep late and relive glory days of childhood by watching reruns of Scooby Doo as opposed to tromping off with friends before the sun came up into cold water or woods in search of wild game. But when a middle-aged woman, in his office for a check-up, remarked how nice and soft his hands were, he confided in a co-worker/friend, who was a male nurse at the hospital, that he might be ready to start hunting ducks after all.

Before firing a single shot, Bubba joined a premiere

duck hunting club with a lease in northern Mississippi. The club was a five-hour drive away, and he only knew one of the other hunting members—his co-worker/friend—but, oh well, it was just money. Besides, it was a promising opportunity to obtain, through a sort of cultural reverse osmosis, some of that masculine mentality that makes the gristle of a tough southern man palatable, if not occasionally delectable.

The day before his first season opened, he arrived at the club's three-bedroom trailer, which came with the lease, and was greeted at the door by his co-worker/friend, the only other club member he knew. As Bubba unloaded his car, with the begrudging help of his doctor-friend and three more hunters already outside to do the "meet and greet", it became apparent that this novice was well prepared for his foray into machismo. Bubba had arrived with a new shotgun, a new pair of waders, and shiny, new boots on his feet. Perched on his completely-bald head was a camouflage, floppy-style hat, so new that club comrades expected to find the tag still dangling, a la Minnie Pearl.

Bubba was well-suited for hunting, he figured, based on the first night at camp. He easily drank as many light beers as the other hunters and shoveled down a plate of something known as "duck hash," while cursing on cue and laughing at every punch-line of every hunting joke told.

"...And he was still out there waiting for that snipe at midnight..." said his co-worker/friend.

"Midnight!" responded Bubba. "Oh, shit, man...you're killing me...I can't take any more, it's making my stomach hurt. That's the funniest fucking thing I've ever heard in my life. Snipe hunting...a riot, man."

The next morning, on the opening day of duck season, Bubba got up early, never once turning on the television, which was wired with a rabbit ear antenna, to see if Scooby Do reruns were on. He dressed in his new, slightly-stiff garb, loaded his unscratched gun before it was time— nobody, however, said a word—and followed his co-worker and new hunting buddies to the field. Minutes after shooting time, birds quacked and flapped and flocked just in front of them. On a nod from his co-worker/friend, he fired a shot, and another, as did his co-worker/friend and the other hunters. Four birds dropped. The sequence was replayed again, and again. Within 45 minutes, the group had killed a legal limit though he was fairly sure no direct hits on ducks came from pellets fired from his gun. But it didn't matter, since, in the elements, his hands were feeling rougher already.

Back at the camp, with most of an entire day remaining ahead, he was told they would not hunt ducks in the afternoon, allowing the birds to settle back into the fields for late, unmolested feeding. Nothing to worry, though. A pay-for-play quail hunt on horseback, with birds raised in pens and released just ahead of their arrival, was scheduled at a nearby plantation. Bubba had never ridden a horse but was told again, no worries, since the swayed-back, rode-hard ponies used at Bronco's Qualified Quail Hunts were said to be like a 40-year-old hooker picked up on Memphis' Beale Street—they could be mounted with ease and made for a slow, comfortable ride.

The two-hour quail hunt went off without a hitch, as much as Bubba knew. His co-worker/friend killed one bird, for which the group was charged $125, and another hunter killed two birds, for which the group was charged $250, and he did not know it was lame that the pen-raised birds never flushed from the ground, even for a brief moment, after scented and pointed by the dogs. He was even proud of himself for well-managing the horse, which hadn't bucked and never walked in the wrong direction.

Back at the camp later that same night, however, the hunting jokes were not nearly as funny as they were the night before, and the light beer and the camp food did not taste nearly so good, for in the crevice of his crack—the half-exposed trough between the anus and the lower back—something felt as if it was crawling and biting and itching and…causing misery. Finally, he could take it no more, exploding in syntax more suitable for a sanitation worker than a surgeon.

"Good, gosh," he said, "something has done crawled up my ass."

Laughter from co-worker/friend and other hunters.

"I'm serious, you dumb ass, duck huntin' mother fuckers. Something has crawled in my ass and somebody is going to have to see what the hell it is."

The co-worker/friend and other hunters had already consumed six beers or more apiece, but they knew better in an all-male camp setting than to easily agree to look at another man's unclothed rear-end. Therefore, nobody volunteered to take a look.

Still, Bubba persisted.

"Okay," his co-worker/friend said. "I'm a nurse. I guess I can take a look. Drop your drawers and bend over."

Bubba unfastened the string of the camouflage "lounge pants" he was wearing, turned his bottom toward his co-worker/friend, pushed pants and boxers down to his knees and bent over, exposing two extremely hairy cheeks.

"No wonder your head has no hair," one hunter remarked. "It all concentrated on your ass."

The co-worker/friend looked closely, but could see nothing.

"Your cheeks are so tightly closed," he said, "it appears

that, instead of a crack, you have a tightly-sealed tomb. If you want me to look, you're going to have to give King Tutankhamen some air."

While still bending over, Bubba placed one hand on his left check and one on his right, pulling each as far apart from the other as he could manage. Exposed was a large, red rash-looking lesion.

"Oh, God," the co-worker/friend uttered, falling backwards and clutching his chest in mock horror.

After composing himself, the affliction was assessed as "chiggers," the pesky mite that bites Southerners in tight bodily places. Never mind that it was late November and 43 degrees outside—a temperature that would send all chiggers into hiding—at this point, the co-worker/friend wasn't thinking like an experienced nurse but one with a six-pack buzz. So he ran back to the hallway bathroom, reached into the medicine cabinet, and retrieved a small bottle of clear liquid.

"This," he told Bubba, "will get rid of those chiggers. Spread those cheeks again and let me put it on."

When his co-worker/friend applied with a tiny brush attached to the tiny lid the strong-smelling medicine to the rash deep in the crevice of Bubba's ultra-hairy cheeks, it stung, badly. Bubba screamed, but three more times on the hour, he asked for the application to reoccur. However,

•
•
•
•
•
•

when he got out of bed the next morning after not sleeping, he urged his co-worker/friend to take another look.

"It ain't gettin' no better," Bubba said. "In fact, it's worse. Much worse."

The co-worker/friend rubbed the sleep crusts from his eyes and became acutely aware of the situation when Bubba dropped his drawers. Absent of alcohol in his system, his co-worker was able to see clearly now.

"Awww, man," co-worker/friend said. "You don't have chiggers! That's a saddle sore. You got a rash from riding that horse. It wouldn't be that big a deal if we hadn't painted it with all that medicine. But now, I don't really know what to do."

Bubba did not return to the hunting camp that year, figuring, I suppose, that he would just get his needed levels of rural ruggedness elsewhere. There were the cowboy boots that he bought and wore to social functions despite the fact that the closest they ever came to manure was the dog-doo he stepped in on the curbside while retrieving his mail as he returned from an early-evening soiree. And there were chamois shirts, "Git'R Done" caps and Lynyrd Skynyrd greatest hits CDs. But the pride and joy, the thing that Bubba was positively sure rubbed off on him the most, where his wheels, a fully-loaded Ford 150 pickup truck, equipped with a 16-disc CD changer.

With four-wheel drive, a super-cab, eight-cylinders and every gadget one could guess, it was the roughest element of his soft-hand façade. There was, of course, no reason that he needed a truck at all, much less one that was so big and so bad that whenever he drove to places like BayBear baseball games, or down to Gulf Shores for a long weekend, young southern men gave approving glances as if he were a member of some secret brotherhood.

He thought at the time of the purchase that the truck made no sense. For three years, he had driven a four-door Volvo sedan that didn't have so much as a cup holder. But, even though the car fit him well, he felt at the grocery store more like a mom, than a man. So when the lease on the Volvo was due to expire, he visited an area Ford dealership just as a look-see. When the salesman backed this particular truck out into the open for him to see, however, he was immediately converted as if a host of Daisy Duke looka-like angels were in the clouds above, singing together a tune, "He's a Ford truck man…" The hymn was so inspirational that, when glancing down to wipe a meek tear from an eye, he thought he saw a new inscription on the bracelet around his wrist.

"What would Toby (Keith) drive?"

Bubba bought the truck and felt instantly more virile, just as every man who spends time in and around vehicular power of the bulging, testosterone kind. It doesn't matter if it's a four-wheel drive flatbed or a rebuilt, 1960s muscle car—the clinging aroma of power and elegant strength and raw beauty are more than enough to overcome the soft sensing of urbanization. It is a trap that I have fallen into myself, purchasing SUVs with a four-wheel drive system that is never, ever engaged. Most of us are unable to resist the temptation of a quick, but ill-advised affair with rugged romance.

There is one particular instance that I recall, in which the desire to obtain brief, natural male performance enhancement, occurred, predictably, on a Tennessee Saturday night. It was summertime, well after the Fourth of July, but weeks before football camps were to convene in the Holy land, a period when the timeless beauty of power collided with the reckless love of men, resulting in an eight-minute, harmonious fling that will long be remembered.

The evening started innocently enough, with a few couples sitting outside, visiting as Southerners are known to do in the days between Memorial and Labor, and discussing the issues of the day in the literal heat of the moment. It was late enough for darkness to blend with the heavy, humid air, creating an enveloping shroud but early enough still that fireflies hovered above the ground. There was a clarity of mind surrounding the group despite the airy haze and nary a whimsical thought verbalized until discussion turned to a car—the always-parked-in-front pride-and-joy of our host, Ryan Crimmins, a business-man and formerly the mayor of tiny-but-pristine Lookout Mountain, Tennessee.

A 1971 Oldsmobile 442, the mayor's collector car was painted light blue and adorned down the middle with two thick, white racing-like stripes. Loaded with an eight-cylinder, 365-horsepower engine, the Olds 442 is known as one of the fastest models of cars ever made available for sale to the American public. It's basically American art on wheels and a reminder of the days when gas was cheap, dashboards were sexy and young, southern men were enam-ored with fast cars. The Olds 442 is also a reminder of what potency was all about before Viagra came along.

"Take two trips around the block with a busty babe in the front seat and the radio blaring and call me in the morning."

Found in 2003 through an internet search by a son about to get a driver's license, Mr. Crimmins' ultimate muscle car was the child-like possession of a laborer living in Eerie, Pennsylvania. The man needed the money for bills and was forced to sell the mint-condition vehicle, parting with it despite tears and a final, passionate rub of the steering wheel. Recognizing the opportunity to purchase a hard-to-find car in near perfect condition, Mr. Crimmins flew into town, made a deal with the man, and drove the vehicle home, turning heads all along the north-toward-home way. Because the car gets only single digit gas mileage per gallon and is a bit loose in handling on the highway at high speeds, the car spends most days in the driveway, exercised with short joy-ride cruising, but its attraction and allure never fails.

On the night at hand, the discussion of the powerful ride and its heyday attributes by a couple of imbibing patio-squatters at the mayor's house yielded an irresistible call. Great cars were built to be driven, after all. A 40-something ex-ballplayer suggested taking a spin. An almost 40-year-old writer was already thinking the very same thing.

"You drive," I said. "I'll ride."

Big Jim—a one-time slugger for North Carolina's Tar Heels, who later played in professional baseball's Double-A Southern League before getting a real job—turned the ignition key, and the engine gave in response a quick, starting growl, before settling into a pulsating throaty murmur. He backed slowly out of the driveway and let the car cruise along on fumes as we fled the mayor's earshot. Minutes later, with the 442 Olds cruising at just 20 miles per hour, Big Jim punched the pedal to the floor, making the tires screech like a colony of demented owls, leaving a quarter-

David Magee

inch of rubber on the road and picking up an additional 40 miles per hour in mere seconds.

We couldn't hide the childish smiles on our grown-men faces.

"Hey, Big Jim," I said. "You think if we took this hot rod downtown, the girls would come running?"

"Sure they would," he said, never hesitating.

Happily married, I did not mean it, of course. It was just the car talking.

But while Big Jim made that fast car screech and squeal in the dark haze of the sultry, summer night, my imagination ran wild. I pictured us driving it off Lookout Mountain into downtown Chattanooga, rumbling through the city's toughest neighborhoods, Big Jim's best wooden bat resting just inches from his fingertips.

Step back, Mr. Policeman. Big Jim will take care of those fellows in that crack house. A few swats here, a few swats there, then we'll be well on our way. Not even Chattanooga's finest could catch us getting away.

"You could do it," I said.

"Yeah, I could," he said.

Before I knew it, however, we had circled back to the mayor's house on the mountain, and it was time to step out of his car and rightfully return the keys to a more responsible party.

.
.
.
.
.
.

"How was the ride?" the mayor asked.

"Great," Big Jim said. "But, just to be on the safe side, you might want to wait a day or two before taking it back out."

Chapter Fourteen

•
•
•
•
•
•

They Smoke While Standing Up

THROUGHOUT THE LATTER half of the 20th century, there was always a silent understanding that the traditional Southern Belle was not exactly what she outwardly portrayed herself to be. The roots of this deception go back to the 1950s and 60s when the young, well-reared girls of Dixie began to experience a sort of nocturnal, social awakening, venturing in the dark of night with trusted friends to places like beer joints in the county, while also experimenting with the physical and metaphysical, and absorbing, and thus, enacting some habits of their more crude male counterparts.

But because these young ladies were often members of such prestigious, higher-brow organizations, such as Delta Delta Delta and Chi Omega, which well-managed their social conscience and public behavior; and because they were taught by conservative mothers previously reared in the South that there were just certain things a girl could not or should not do, under any circumstances, they rather closely adhered to a self-policed, confining code.

If they smoked, which almost all of them did at least some of the time, they were taught to only do so while sitting down, preferably with crossed legs, a straight spine and a chin pointing slightly upward. They were also taught, among many lessons, to never call boys on the telephone, to avoid the appearance of sweating in public, to not wear white shoes or carry a white handbag before Easter or after Labor Day, to never drink excessively in public, to avoid eating large amounts of food in front of anyone, to never curse out loud, and to avoid any sexual dialogue with the opposite sex at all times.

By adhering to such puritan rules of behavior, the Southern Belle evolved into a kind of double-persona being, flaunting herself wildly at times in improper places, only to see it all evaporate, as if someone took a giant eraser to their actions, through social repentance, by abiding by the expected and demanded code of conduct for the Southern Belle. As a prime example, there is one woman I know, who claims to have arrived as a sorority pledge at Ole Miss from South Mississippi as a virgin. She had been raised properly, she said, and while in high school worked hard to protect her innocence, as well as her reputation.

There were some brushes with disaster, she recalled, like the time she was parking early in the evening with her boyfriend on a dirt road on her father's farm. For weeks, her boyfriend had been begging and begging to unfasten her clothes. She refused to wholly give in, but, recognizing that a compromise might be needed to keep him hanging around, she relented, just a bit, allowing him to flop one boob completely out of her shirt and bra. Although he expressed initial dissatisfaction at the compromise, he apparently decided to give that one boob all the attention he could muster, sucking her left nipple so loudly and furiously it looked like he was nine years old again and had just been give a red, white and blue atomic bomb popsicle at the county fair.

The attention was enough, however, that her mind wandered. She did not hear a car drive up, and, for a moment, she did not hear the tap, tap, tapping on the car window. Finally, her eyes focused on the window enough to see her father's face peering in.

"Daddy!"

She screamed so loudly that her boyfriend jumped from his perch, bumping his head on the car roof, completely exposing her wet, slobbery left breast to her father. She blushed, in the tradition of any belle, fastened her shirt, and left with her father, who never mentioned a word about the episode—then, or later.

At Ole Miss, her considerable good belle behavior earned an invitation to one of the universities best sororities. After initiation, she remained true to herself, as well as the Alpha, the Omega and the Father, all the way through to graduation. She never had sex on a pool table at the downtown bar while her best friend, slugging a beer, looked the other way and pretended not to notice, and she never performed oral sex on a guy in the living room of his rented house while he strummed the guitar non-stop, and she never went to the infirmary, crying and covering her left eye because it was badly irritated after being splashed with squirting semen, and, she never smoked cigarettes while standing up, much less hanging upside down on monkey bars at the city park at three in the morning, with classes due to start in five hours.

By abiding by the rules of belledom, she married well, made a good name and home for herself back in South Mississippi, and she had a daughter of her own, Mary Madelyn, who was reared according to the same principles of yore. She, too, went to Ole Miss, enrolling as a freshman in 2005, and pledged the very same sorority as her mother. In the 21st century, however, much had certainly changed for the young, Southern woman, the mother quickly noticed.

While helping Mary Madelyn move into the dorm on the first day, for example, she could not help but gawk at the bare bellies, overly-tight bras and thongs slightly exposed from the tops of low-riding jeans appearing at every glance. Almost every girl carried items from their car to their room while simultaneously talking on the their cell phones, often to—gasp—boys they had dialed, blurting out words that she used to say only when the sun went down and fewer people were around. After Mary Madelyn was all moved into the room, they went out for a late-night dinner at a restaurant. There were a number of upper class students gathered around the bar, huddling like penguins, and almost every standing girl among them held a lit cigarette in her hand. Others sat together at tables, the girls hunkering over plates of pizza and pasta, while others traipsed together with boys on the sidewalk in front of the establishment, swashbuckling in short skirts, tall boots and the seductive swagger of a vixen.

It became apparent to the mother that young, southern girls of the 21st century had shucked the rules and regulations of being a belle, opting instead to be themselves, in the open, at all times, even when raising a little hell. If they wanted to call a boy, they simply dialed one up; if they want to curse, they didn't fear doing it loudly and unapologetically.

The fall semester went fine for Mary Madelyn, minus the two minor-in-possession-of-alcohol citations she received from the Oxford police, along with one for public exposure related to a urinating incident at 11:30 on a Saturday night in a parking lot just off the town square. When she came home for Christmas, her parents found a large, unidentified stain on the passenger floorboard of her six-month old car, as well as her 23 extra pounds of flab, and several holes conspicuously burned in low-cut, v-neck sweaters. In spite of these discoveries, the 2.65 grade point average and the impending initiation into sisterhood made for a time worth celebrating. Mary Madelyn was encouraged to invite friends to her home for the holidays, so her parents could meet and get to know them, and four girls from towns scattered throughout the South accepted, arriving five days after Christmas.

On the first night, the woman and her husband took the girls 30 miles north to Jackson for dinner at a popular Brazilian-style steakhouse—the kind where a waiter shows up every few minutes or so with another meat to try. The husband was full after three rounds, but managed to hang in for a fourth; same for his wife. The girls, however, continued raising their hands, again and again, soliciting more chops, more loin, and more kabobs. On the way home, they sat very still in the car, saying nothing and doing little more than constantly clicking text messages on the phone. At the house, they filed in one by one into the bathroom, keeping the tub running. By the time each had exited, they seemed to have a new-found, less than full energy, pledging to go out for the night.

Not more than 15 minutes after the girls left the house, however, the telephone rang. It was the local police. The girls had been stopped during a routine traffic corral. When the daughter had rolled down the window, marijuana smoke billowed from the car. They were taken in, and the call was made, but charges would not be filed. The father picked them up at the station and brought them home as they smacked on gum and clicked more messages on the phone the entire way. After explaining to the mother that they were merely experimenting with something someone else had given them, they asked the unthinkable.

"Can we go back out tonight?"

Because they were dressed up so cute, all ready to go, the mother relented. Shortly after they were gone, for the second time, the father and mother sat down on the couch to catch their breath from the whirlwind of the evening's activity. The father felt something under his leg, reached under a cushion to feel what it might be, retrieving a cell phone that one of the girl's had left behind.

"It's not Mary Madelyn's," the mother said. "Hers is bigger than that. It must belong to one of the other girls."

The father handed the mother the fun in hopes that she could determine the rightful owner. The mother turned it on, hoping to find some clues imbedded inside. She clicked on the "messages sent" folder first, figuring the girl might have pinged her mother or typed in a contact name that would yield a clue. She began to read. Her brow furrowed, and she squirmed slightly in her chair.

"Oh, my," she told her husband.

"What?"

"Oh, my," she repeated.

"What?"

"Listen to this," she said, before reading off several entries out loud. *"You are too hot. I'm thinking of your penis. It makes me so wet. I want to grab it.. Are you thinking of me?"*

"Dear God," the man said. "Is that real?"

"I'm afraid so," the mother said. "All these were sent earlier tonight, on our way home from dinner.

"I want to feel you..." the mother said, reading another passage.

"Stop!" the father said. "You've got to stop. It is starting to turn me on."

They shut the phone off and, exasperated, went to bed. At about half past noon the next day, the girls slithered out of bed, down the stairs and into the kitchen where they were eating lunch.

"What time did y'all get in last night?" the mother asked.

"Oh," said Mary Madelyn, "about two."

"Well," the mother said, "which one of you didn't have a phone? We found one, and expected you were missing it."

"That's mine," one of the girls spoke up. "I'm so glad you found it. Where was it?"

"On the couch in the den," the mother said.

"Cool," said the girl. "Mary Madelyn's battery died on the way home from dinner last night and I handed her mine to use. She was messaging some boy back and forth she had met at the bar the night before. She didn't even know his name, just his phone number. I asked her later where the phone was, but she didn't remember where she had left it."

Chapter Fifteen

.
.
.
.
.
.

The Ivory-billed Woodpecker is Back
—But Not for Long

YEARS AGO, A PERSONAL FAVORITE place to hunt for wildlife, hang out, and remind myself that I was not the dumbest of lads walking the earth was the flatlands of Arkansas. Hovering beside the mighty Mississippi River, the eastern side of the Natural State is a geography both blessed and cursed by highly-fertile soil, which is quite suitable for the abundant production of crops but meets the expecting eye in the harshest of manners. Similarly, wildlife flourishes, reaching a majestic potential when unmolested, yet the same can't be said for the human population, often hindered by rural isolation and the considerable lack of higher education. In other words, for the outdoorsman, it is utopia; for the humanitarian, it is a social case study. This is a story of what happens when the two worlds collide.

Not one who grew up hunting, or spending excessive time in the rugged outdoors, I was taught to deer hunt and duck hunt in the Arkansas delta region by one of the finest men I know, a farmer who could have done anything he wanted professionally, but who chose to live from the land that he loved. Whenever I wanted to go duck hunting, he took me, each time exhibiting the meaning of respect and management. We never killed more than a limit, with the exception of one or two occasions by accident, and we never fired a shot a minute before, or a minute after, legally-mandated shooting times. And, whenever I wanted to go deer hunting, he took me, explaining that small bucks should be left alone and that a doe should not be killed until the precise day the law allowed.

Unfortunately, my tutor passed away far before his time, leaving me in somewhat of a lurch hunting-wise. Not wanting to quit and give up my new hobby and passion, I continued for some years traveling to the area when opportunity called, taking to the fields with a myriad of others. One of the more interesting of my hunting compatriots was a 19-year-old, sandy-blonde haired, native of Stuttgart, the Arkansas town of just more than 10,000 residents billed as the duck hunting capital of the world. Having quit school in the tenth grade because it was too difficult and time-consuming, Joe Don "JD" Jones was a full-time hunter, who supported himself and paid his year-round bills cutting grass during the summer months.

At first acquaintance, JD came across as a young man who would be a sophomore at The University of Arkansas at Fayetteville and in a good fraternity. It did not take long, however, for him to reveal through colloquial English that he once shot a 10-point buck in a neighbor's front yard in the mid-morning, that he had just one testicle—one really, really big testicle—and that he was usually unable to remember how to spell what they once told him in school he had—"dyslexia." When it came to the outdoors, however, JD was anything intellectually challenged. He seemed to know everything one could know about the habits of wildlife and how to best stalk and kill it. As for rules, regulations and general gentlemanly demeanor in regard to such, well, those were different matters—something that I learned on our first days out in the field together.

I was set up to hunt with JD by a friend of a friend who knew I was looking for an outdoors partner, so I didn't know him before showing up to meet at 4:45 in the parking lot of a greasy-spoon breakfast diner on the outskirts of town. Pulling up, I made notice of the more than two dozens pickup trucks filling the lot, wondering how I would identify my hunting partner. But within a minute, a truck pulled beside me and a window rolled down. I peered inside, seeing JD display a broad smile that was punctuated by a lumpy protrusion on the lower lip. He leaned out the window and spit toward the ground a long streak of brown saliva.

"You ready to kill some ducks?"

"Absolutely," I said. "You think the hunting will be any good?

"Hard to say," he said. "It was clear most of the night, so them tappers have been a feedin' all night. It's fairly cold, though, which oughta help. We'll just have to go out there and see."

JD gave me the motion to follow him, and I pulled behind him as he departed the lot. For 15 miles we rode through the dark of night before pulling off on a gravel road. Rabbits feeding before the sun came up flared from the left and the right all the way down as we crunched our way another two miles. Finally, his hand appeared from the driver's side window, telling me to slow. He pulled over to the side of the road, closely hovering near the edge of a ditch and cut off the engine. I did the same. He walked over to my SUV and I rolled down my window, opening my mouth to speak.

"Shhhhhh," he said. "Listen."

Quaaaack, quack, quack, quack, quack….quuaaaack, quack, quack, quack, quack.

"Somebody's a callin' you from over in that field."

We threw on our waders, fastened our jackets, grabbed our guns and shells and walked about 300 yards down a dim and un-graveled dirt road, before turning and walking another 100 yards or so down a rice field levee that was covered on both sides by thigh-deep water and was barely traversable because so many feeding ducks had walked over it, wearing down the sides to slick mud. Throughout the moon-lit walk, hen-mallards could be heard chattering in the background. When we reached what appeared to be a tall lump of field grass, JD kicked with his left foot and the lid to an in-ground hunting pit slid open.

"Climb in," he said. "It's almost shootin' time."

At 28 minutes before sunrise—legal shooting time—two mallard drakes and a hen whirred overhead. JD reached for his duck call, and started quacking, trying with all his might to hail them back our way. One duck listened, made the turn, and the other two followed.

"That's some shit right there, ain't it?"

"Yeah, it is," I replied.

As the ducks neared, JD closed the lid to the blind so that we had just a crack to peek from. He kept blowing his call, telling me between guttural exhales to get ready.

.
.
.
.
.
.

Before I expected it, he flung the lid completely open, giving the command.

"Shoot that one to the right."

Aiming my 12-gauge shotgun with just enough lead, I squeezed the trigger, then watched the mallard drake fall from the sky, splashing into the water.

"Nice shot."

"Looks like it is still swimming," I said.

"Yep, better go get it."

For 40 yards, I waded through the water, only to find that the duck was still alive, fleeing on water. I started to run, hearing JD's laughter from the pit. Finally, I caught the duck, grabbing it by the neck. To kill it, I tried as my mentor had done, holding the duck's head and swinging its body in a fast circle to wring its neck. Perhaps because I did not really want to kill the duck in such a manner and, therefore, didn't do the trick with required vigor, it flipped and flopped throughout my walk back to the pit, still alive.

"Don't you know how to kill a damn duck?" JD said.

"Well, yeah, but..."

"Hand it to me."

JD rose from his seat, clasped the duck with both his left and right hands, and placed the crown of its head into his mouth, between his upper and lower teeth.

Crunch.

He had bitten so that the duck's skull crushed into its brain, inflicting immediate death and sending shivers up my back.

JD removed the duck from his mouth, looked up and me and smiled a smile that country boys call "a shit-eatin' grin." To my dismay, blood ran from the corner of the left side of his mouth, down to his chin.

"That," he said, "is how you kill a duck...essept, I got a little brain running in my mouth and that don't taste good. Try not to do that. You just want it to go crunch, not crunch then splat."

Four of the other five ducks we killed later that morning died of the same fate. After so many times, the act lost its oddity, but I do recall thinking at some point between the first and last bite that this is exactly the type of situation made for Jeff Foxworthy's famous line, "You might be a redneck if..."

If there was any doubt that JD was qualified as a redneck by Foxworthy standards, it was removed on a subsequent duck hunting trip back to the same field. Arriving in similar fashion, it was not ducks we heard quacking upon arrival, but geese squawking loudly. With enough moonlight shining across the field, we could see snows and blues numbering in the thousands sitting on the water, feeding in the field we were about to hunt.

-
-
-
-
-

"Well, this ain't no good," JD spat. "The ducks won't never come in here with all these geese."

We made as much noise as possible climbing into the pit, bumping our guns against its walls, but it didn't matter. The geese weren't disturbed. We waited 30 minutes past shooting time, until sunrise, and knew that something had to be done to get the geese out of the field if we wanted any of the ducks flying overhead to land. JD's solution was that we would both shoot our guns three times, emptying all loaded shells. If we could reload in time, he said, we might as well shoot as many geese as we could, before they fly out of range. Since it was goose season, this seemed reasonable enough to me.

"I don't really like to eat goose, though," I told him.

"So," he said. "There's too many of 'em anyway. Just get as many as you can."

On command, we fired our guns. Sure enough, geese by the thousands took to the air. It was an amazing sight, one that I admired until remembering that I could reload and fire. JD, of course, beat me to it, and I watched him fire one, two, then three shots after hearing him utter an expletive.

"Mother fucker," he said.

POW, POW, POW.

"What?"

"Look," he said.

Struggling to fly 40 yards overhead was the biggest white goose I had ever seen. It bellowed a funny noise, stretched out a long, odd-looking neck, and folded its wings, splashing into the water.

"Mother fucker."

JD jumped out of the pit and ran toward the bird with me pursuing behind him, soaking up his water spray. The goose didn't try to swim away but floated partially in and out of the water, like a marooned ship. The goose was dead, except, it did not appear to be a goose at all.

"What is that?" I asked nervously.

"That," JD said, "is a trumpeter swan. I've only seen one before. But they migrate. They get in flying with these geese and head South with 'em. Then, they head back north with 'em.

"There ain't many left in North America. I think it's an endangered species."

"What?" I said. "What did you say? Endangered species?"

"Yep, I don't think there's a whole lot of 'em left."

"You mean to tell me you just shot, on purpose, a bird on the endangered species list? Are you kidding me! What in God's name were you thinking?"

"I ain't never seen one up close," said Arkansas' finest. "How else could I? It was flyin', so I shot it.

"Pretty, ain't she?"

When I first heard in 2005 that someone claimed to have sighted in Arkansas the year before an ivory-billed woodpecker, presumed extinct for the previous 50 years, I was naturally concerned. Spotted in eastern Arkansas, in an area close to where JD killed the Trumpeter Swan and where dozens, if not hundreds of other "outdoorsmen" held the same appreciation of wildlife as he, I feared the woodpecker which flew back from the dead may have a short-lived resurrection. I mean, there are people in that neck of the woods —obviously—that will shoot anything. The black bear, for instance, was all but exterminated by the predecessors of JD and others, before the government stepped in with laws just harsh enough for the bears to survive. The white-tailed deer was in a similar predicament in the Natural State during the early 1900s, and my buddy JD was doing his part to eradicate the trumpeter swan.

Seriously, what chance does the ivory-billed woodpecker have?

Because of this familiarity with the region and its people, I closely followed the story involving a supposed sighting of an extinct woodpecker. From the beginning, I was mesmerized by news accounts that scientists had confirmed that America's largest woodpecker, the ivory-billed, lived in the "Big Woods" of the eastern, Arkansas flatlands. It was as if Elvis had been videotaped in Idaho and determined to be alive and okay. Here was this bird, among the most beloved of any birds to have ever flown in the world, vanished from man for half a century, only to be found flying among the trees once again.

I will admit that once I learned more about the story, I began to have some suspicions that the big bird was actually back. Some of the best scientists and bird watching specialists in the country were confirming the sighting as fact, but an episode of 60 Minutes left me with more questions than answers. For starters, after a suspected initial sighting was made in 2004, a year-long expedition to obtain substantial evidence of the bird's existence resulted in only a four second video as proof. The footage was shown on 60 Minutes and my face turned red with embarrassment for these scientists—supposedly experts—putting their reputation on the line for a four second video that was so blurry, you couldn't even tell if it was a bird or flying squirrel zipping across the background, much less one that had been supposedly extinct for 50 years.

Ivory-billed woodpecker?

I doubt it.

In the time it takes you to read this sentence, the bird had already entered the camera's view and left. What's

.
.
.
.
.
.

worse, the other men in the boat didn't even see it at the time.

"A large black and white woodpecker flew off a tree," said University of Arkansas at Little Rock professor David Luneau, who caught the flying bird on his camcorder.

One might assume the large bird was a pileated woodpecker, but when the blurry film was analyzed closely, the bird in question was said to have five crucial characteristics that distinguished it as an ivory-billed. The evidence eluded me, even after seeing the close-ups, but the confirmation was ultimately made by experts associated with the Cornell Laboratory of Ornithology in New York and The Nature Conservancy.

After watching the tape, I couldn't see how they really knew the difference. The men in the boat are floating along and chatting, probably about why Razorback football coach Houston Nutt can't win big games, when all of a sudden a big bird swoops by, out of the men's sight but caught on the video camera. It is only later, when experts review the video that they conclude it was the previously extinct ivory-billed woodpecker flying by.

I know, I know. A team of experts had essentially lived in the woods for a year without laying eyes on it, but now, with a blurry video, the bird is back from the dead? Hasn't football already taught us that instant replay doesn't always make for the right calls? Even back in the 1970s, Big Foot and UFOs boasted more substantial evidence. I recall seeing a completely clear video of Big Foot during my childhood. There was some sort of special on television, and the camera panned to a giant footprint in the mud. Another clip showed a big, furry creature running in the background, before lumbering out of sight. I could easily believe that was Big Foot, just as I could easily believe people in New Mexico who claimed to have witnessed unidentified flying objects. They simply saw things that weren't clearly identifiable...

But a four second blurry video of a woodpecker? My gut said no, this can't be true, but, in the end, my brain overruled. While I don't know much, I have enough sense to know a graduate of Ole Miss should never question someone associated with Cornell. Also, bird watchers seem like types who should be trusted. If these folks say the ivory-billed woodpecker is back, then I have no choice but to believe them. So, I quit questioning the validity of evidence, and began celebrating with the rest of the world that a treasured bird was gracing the earth once again.

My hopefulness was short-lived, however, when I remembered that the ivory-billed woodpecker squeaking by in one of the most dangerous areas for wildlife known in the world—backwoods Arkansas. Perhaps it was true,

•
•
•
•
•
•

I surmised, that the bird was spotted in the "Big Woods" in 2004. But even though the sighting remained a secret worldwide, local gossip might have let the word out in the flatlands. JD lives not 25 miles from there, and so do several of his hunting buddies, not to mention hundreds of others just like them.

I could just see it now, understanding why the group of some 50 experts and field biologists got nothing more than a blurry videotape in a year of looking. JD had heard about the bird, called a buddy, and floated a boat back into the woods before the high-brow woodpecker search expedition ever got started. That big, beautiful ivory-billed wood-pecker lighted on a tree. JD flipped the safety, took aim, and squeezed the trigger.

BAM.

"Mother fucker."

"What is it JD?"

"That, my boy, was the last ivory-billed woodpecker known to man."

"What? Isn't that bird extinct?"

"It is now."

"Well, damn...why did you shoot it?"

"Cause, I ain't never seen one before."

Chapter Sixteen

.
.
.
.
.

Adapting to Change, Southern Style

JUST LAST YEAR, I MADE the startling discovery that I was about to pass the point of age which signifies, in all likelihood, that I am more than halfway dead. That's what the statistics show us anyway. I found a web site that uses a formula to determine remaining life expectancy when such individual characteristics including age, weight, genetics, and amount of weekly exercise are input. Curious to know the prognostication of my time left on earth with a milestone birthday approaching, I entered my data, even though it felt more like appraising the value of a used car.

Year of make: 1965; mileage: excessive; special features: runs well under pressure; problems: no major ones detectable, but there is slight a chipping of the paint on the roof

•
•
•
•
•
•

and a gimpy right rear wheel base; general condition: fair. One click of the mouse and presto! The number appeared soberly before my eyes.

Average trade-in value: 75 years.

I was completely surprised that the result stirred any internal anxiety at all. For many years I have been completely confident and outspoken that the approach of my 40th birthday would be a non-factor; the prelude to a ho-hum event; just another day and another number. Throughout my adult life, many of my friends have been older than I, which helps make me feel young. This idea of personal youthfulness occurred partly by accident and partly due to the fact that, since I had children at a young age, my peer set has always run a little higher. Also, I've been able to maintain an energetic approach to life, avoiding the stuck-in-the-mud tendencies of ideas and trends that accompany some of us geezers in age.

My 17-year-old and I, for example, have iPods loaded with exactly the same songs. I'm proud to know that The Cranberries are more than just a Thanksgiving meal garnish, and I will admit having attended an alternative rock concert by myself within the last two years, though there is no need to mention the fact that I left between sets, had searing eyes from wave upon wave of cigarette smoke, and couldn't hear properly out of my left ear for the next three days. I also reassess my wardrobe every few years and am not afraid of a little caffeine in the evening (as long as it's the weekend) and will eat pizza and sub-sandwiches any day of the week. Just try me.

Though more than anything, the fact that each year I have lived has been more enjoyable than the one before has given me the impression that age is much more a blessing than it is the methodical deterioration of the human body. With each passing year, I'm smarter, with more freedoms and people with which to share the things I love. So, when friends have talked through the years about trepidation in turning 40, 50, or even 60, I have generally scoffed: "Get over it." But when I inputted my information on the web site and clicked the mouse to see my life expectancy pop up at 75, I realized that, upon my 40th birthday later in the month, I would officially be on the statistical down slope of life, with less time remaining than I have already lived.

I should have seen it coming. At the dawn of age 20, I was energetic, if not robust. Still in college, chasing the girl of my dreams at Ole Miss, there was a swagger in my step, and I thrived off the young man's ability to stay up late, get up early, and do it all over again. Same for when I turned the age of 30, launching into an era in which I explored the world enough to know that my hometown was not, in fact, the center of the universe and continued

.
.
.
.
.

playing full-court basketball at every opportunity. As the 40th year approached, however, invitations to the big party began to spring up in every direction. There was the onset of the dreaded male hair mutation, in which it flees from the head, only to re-sprout in the oddest of new places.

Yes, I guess my ears do need a trim.

And there was expansion in areas where fat cells are stored. First, they began to gather around my waist; then, they found it was easy to congregate in areas farther up the trunk. Being a bald man is one thing; being bald with breasts is another. Worst of all, many joints and formerly well-working parts of my body now ached and refused to operate as they were intended, causing a general lack of flexibility that fiendishly hounds an active and hopeful man's lifestyle. In spite of it all, though, I still saw my glass as half full as the months passed and my 40th birthday neared.

However, armed with information from a seemingly reliable web site, I was forced to face the fact that my glass was actually more than half empty. Certainly, my reported life expectancy is just an aggregate of all the men good and bad that have died before me. I could easily live longer than the age of 75. But the statistical reality is that the odds are against me that the prognostication will prove to be more right than wrong, leaving me clinging on the short end of the life stick.

With time no longer on my side, I was forced to take an assessment of my mutated life, analyzing who I had become, how I was impacting others around me, and whether the weaknesses of the new me outweighed the strengths. I was able to see that—amid all my increasing ailments and oddities, from retreating muscle mass to increasingly nuanced phobias of like telephone calls and crowded, public places—good things had emerged as well. Yes, I am strangely different from who I was 20 years ago, but I'm also more open-minded and more tolerant of all types of people. I am able to think, as well as create, more broadly than ever before, just as I am able to appreciate the fine qualities of life, such as a good glass of wine, a walk along a mountain top or the exceptional playing of any type of music, hackneyed as that all may be.

And the same has happened in the 21st century South, which has changed beyond recognition from the place where my parents grew up and has even transformed from the place I knew and experienced growing up in the 1960s, 70s and 80s. Therefore, there are moments when, like my own personal evolution, I begin to worry over what this region has become and how much life remains in its collective identity. No longer as isolated, perfunctory and predictable as it once was, nor as black and white, the region has changed into a kind of gathering of flavors

.
.
.
.
.

on one geographical dish that, individually, remain very distinct and strong, some to the point of pungency, but together they mix like black-eyed peas and ketchup—it never seems exactly right, but it goes down just fine.

The result is quite a social study, which distinguishes us new denizens of Dixie with stories and idiosyncrasies that might be worth crying over if they weren't so laughable. For example, one might question how a land—where blacks and whites still struggle after so many years to get along, where the majority of residents are eating themselves into the size of parade floats, and where women are turning increasingly to a killer drug for stamina—could be considered agreeable. It is certainly accurate to say that the new, new South, more than ever before, is a paradox in itself, in which contemporary tastes and ideals battle against age-old traditions. But as with my aging, ever-changing body, saggy skin, gimpy knees, balding head and all, there have been benefits in mutation and rewards from incongruity.

Consider Atlanta, the region's largest city. My metropolitan neighbor, some 120 miles away, sprawls and envelopes the central Georgia landscape like an amoeba with a bad chest cold, absorbing millions in its blobbing wake, but it unquestionably has become the capital of our redneck nation, large enough in body and spirit that it is the home to the world's most trusted news network, comedian Jeff

Foxworthy, and the hip-hop group OutKast. There is black government, black aristocracy and black millionaires, but, as one writer once noted, there is also a "great encircling wealth and true power of white Atlanta" which can and does, "get by quite well without the black-run city center." The factions have learned, though, for the most part, to coexist, allowing commerce, cultural and big ideas to emerge from the bloated metropolis.

How this happened dates back to the middle part of the 20th century when people of all races, looking for big-time opportunity in a place that also offered small-town feel, flocked to the city. Many prospered, including both blacks and whites, who took advantage of a fast-moving urban work environment and a pay scale that was higher than other southern cities. Businesses grew strong, and as some branched out globally, they became more inclusive. Life outside the office evolved into a suburban flair that could best be described as a blend between Foxworthy and Woody Allen.

"You might be a redneck if…you read chapters from *The Blackwell Dictionary of Modern Social Thought* while sitting on the toilet and wearing nothing but calf-length camouflage socks."

Some moments, it was all boot, scoot and boogie; others, the cosmopolitan edginess was unmistakable. This unique combination of multicultural attraction, economic growth and individual opportunity culminated in Atlanta's emergence as the centerpiece of the new South. The city flexed its new-found muscle, and the Olympics—no, that's not the circus—came to town. The once-lowly Braves of Major League Baseball began to win and somehow ended up as America's team, in spite of fans in the 1990's having to endure then-owner Ted Turner and his then-wife Jane Fonda tomahawk chop themselves silly. World class museums, shopping centers and restaurants flourished, as did the advanced public transportation system, which nobody uses. Now, there is even an unreasonably large downtown aquarium. Built upon the generous strength of Arthur Blank, the Home Depot co-founder who also owns the improved-but-still-can't-get-to-the Super Bowl-no-matter-what Falcons, it features a living, oxygen-breathing whale, which is any aquarium's gold standard of shock and awe.

The pock marks that resulted from this transformation are that, as the city morphed from an overgrown, sprawling southern town into an American megopolis, it became a place which honestly embodied told and retold jokes, like the one that says there are so many one-way streets in the city, the only way to get out of the downtown area is "to turn around and start over when you reach Greenville, South Carolina," or, the one that says "the falling of one rain drop causes all traffic to immediately cease; so will daylight savings time and a girl applying eye shadow across the street, or a flat tire three lanes over."

To find Atlanta's aquarium, visitors are going to have to navigate traffic that is among the most stifling in the world. My friends, and yours, the same ones who once flocked there during the dawning of the new, new south, are now working overtime to find ways to flee it. The hourlong commute each way is taking a toll and many residents are getting that queasy, claustrophobic feeling trying to conduct daily life among the metropolitan area's booming population that numbers close to five million. It has gotten so bad that one couple who lives in the Buckhead area of Atlanta left their house on a Friday night in December for a Christmas party which was just more than two miles away, but after not moving more than 400 yards in 45 minutes, they had little choice but to give up and go back home; so much for the yuletide spirit.

Making matters worse for those caught within the strangulating confines of the 285 loop is that the opportunities that once abounded are getting harder to find; crime is on the rise; those wonderful perks like major league sports tickets are getting more expensive; and the Braves, while continuing to win during the regular season, can't seem to recall the keys to victory in the playoffs—Ted? Jane? Where are you?

•
•
•
•
•
•

Also, visiting Atlanta, for the other southerners who just want a glimpse of what life is like in the royal palace, is another story altogether. I make the drive occasionally and still don't know if it takes me two or four hours to get there. And my subconscious mind so loathes the notion of smothering encapsulation that on an early-morning trip to the Atlanta-Hartsfield Airport last year, I was an hour toward Birmingham before I noticed on the car's GPS map that I was traveling in the wrong direction. Once at the airport, almost two hours late and two flights missed, it took another hour or more to navigate security, and all I wanted was to be anywhere but there.

Still, there are other times when I'm in Atlanta, and I look around and realize that it represents this spirit of everything this oft-twisted land called the South is all about in the 21st century. A big-city collection of redneck and soul, with an overriding flavor of small-town, spiced with a pinch of misunderstanding and confusion, it tries desperately to hold onto what it once was, but in the end, the city cannot help embracing what it has become. For this reason, it is a place, like the larger south it embodies as the de facto capital of Dixie, that I very much want to loathe, yet cannot help but love.

• • • • •

Acknowledgements

A VERY SPECIAL THANK YOU for this work goes, above all, to friend, author and fellow newspaper columnist Celia Rivenbark. The first time I read her work in book form, I knew that my calling was to bring a male version of her southern literistic rambling to print. When I gave her an early glimpse of the work in progress, she raved in review and I knew there was no looking back. She's one of the best at articulating the voice of the south and I am very grateful to both her ability and abidance.

I also have deep gratitude for my wife, Kent Rasco Magee, who pushed me to become a writer when doing so probably made no sense and who has supported me along the way at times when doing so probably made no sense.

Her belief, I suppose, has been that an uncomfortable life which yields contribution is better lived than a comfortable life which yields only full hands.

Others who deserve specific mention are Jefferson Press editor Henry Oehmig, who added meaningful touches here, and there, and my friends and employees of Chattanooga's Rock Point Books. Store co-owner Albert Waterhouse also deserves special thanks for it is friends and daring readers like he who make the book such a delectable and redeeming treat.

Finally, Chattanooga Times Free Press Publisher and Editor Tom Griscom is high on my list of those to acknowledge, along with a list of friends who have offered profound and steadfast support along the way. These include, in no particular order, Boofie and Ryan Crimmins; Mike and Amy Brooks; Craig and Terri Holley; John and Marty Dunbar; Charlie and Lisa Brock; and Scott and Alexis Probasco.